I0147147

Maybe Tomorrow...

By Steve Haydock

PANIC
PRESS

www.panic-press.com

A Panic Press Book

Copyright © Steve Haydock

All rights reserved. No part of this publication may be reproduced, stored in a retrieval system, or transmitted in any form or by any means, electronic, mechanical,, photocopy, recording or otherwise, without prior written permission of the copyright owner. Nor can it be circulated in any form of binding or cover other than that in which it is published and without similar condition including this condition being imposed on a subsequent purchaser.

ISBN 978-0-9564831-2-6

Panic Press

The Meridian

Station Square

Coventry CV1 2FL

This book is also available in e-book format, details of which are available at www.panic-press.com

Maybe Tomorrow…

This book was written in 2010, and is based on the diaries I wrote in 1992 during my time as a volunteer soldier in the conflict in the former Yugoslavia. The rest of the story is from memory and can only apologise if some of the details are hazy.

I would like to take this opportunity to thank my wife Louise for all the time she patiently spent typing out my handwritten manuscript, and for just putting up with me! Also special thanks to my publisher: 'Panic-Press', for leading me in the direction to getting this book successfully published and 'out there'.

Finally I would like to dedicate this book to all those who I have proudly served alongside in the 1st Battalion of The Queens Lancashire Regiment, and the 2nd Battalion of 108 Brigade HVO who either fell in action or are no longer with us. Rest In Peace my friends. Duty done.

Steve Haydock

Blackpool, October 2011.

1.

I was 15 years old, or should I say young when I joined the British Army. Fifteen years and 46 days on the 24th August 1972. Only weeks before I had been a schoolboy who had left as early as you could back then, I had left a good education but from a school where I did not really belong. I was one of two government grant boys, given a chance to be educated at Arnold Boy's Grammar school in Blackpool. A chance, some may say, I was foolish to throw away, but when you are from a poor working class family you tend to stand out among the better off kids of Solicitor's, Bankers and Doctor's - I certainly did! I had to wear the obligatory grey suit and cap or the green blazer, cap and trousers, which along with the required sets of sports and gym kits stretched my parent's finances to the limit and beyond, even with the education grant. Each year I got my new elbow patches and repaired trousers as the other boy's uniforms were replaced. It didn't help either being called out after school assembly to go and collect my free dinner tickets - which I promptly sold on the school black market! In fact I disliked that school greatly, except on Friday's. This was the day as part of the school curriculum; when we all turned up at school in our designated cadet uniforms. On Friday afternoons, we would drill and train with the school's combined cadet force. I was put into the army cadets, although I had originally applied to join the air cadets, as both of my parents were ex-RAF, I thought I should have had a good or above average chance of being accepted, obviously not! No 'urchins' in the air cadets, who were themselves, looked down on by the sea cadets - only the army cadets for you Haydock! Those days, or afternoons, were my days, the one day I didn't slink off home early out of the back fire door. At the age of fourteen they even let me go on exercise with them, going to Jurby camp on the Isle of Man for two weeks and I loved it. Even if I was running around in oversize battledress uniform, wearing a beret fit to land a squadron on and dragging around my .303 Lee Enfield rifle that was bigger than me. It gave me the taste for army life!

So, at the age of 15, I escaped school to enter the real army, or so I thought! I walked through the gates of the Infantry Junior Leaders Battalion at Park Hall Camp in Oswestry, Shropshire, to a new life. A very definite shock to my system was about to occur for the next two and a half years. I was among over two hundred new recruits to arrive that day; all assigned to the 7 platoons of Z (recruit) company, and I was to join Harding platoon. The buildings were wooden spider blocks, bleak, bare and cold; each room contained 24 steel lockers and beds. For the next three months we were taught to drill, dress, eat and breathe the Army. Cold dark mornings of 5am reveilles followed by endless 'beastings' on the drill square, to pounding along the country roads or scrambling over assault courses and circuit training in the gym, they were hard and gruelling days. The evenings were spent on correctly setting out your equipment and clothing in the lockers, sorting, cleaning and ironing your kit for the next day, and bumper polishing the floors of your rooms until they gleamed. Midnight brought sleep, followed five hours later by the same again. As each week went by, the Platoons became smaller as people decided the Army was not for them and they left. Bullying was also a major factor for the decline, although not exactly encouraged by the adult regular Army instructors it was either overlooked or just called 'character building'. This went on throughout all my junior training, often people who were not as quick, or as strong as the main groups were singled out by the instructors and we were all told 'this man will let you down if you don't get a grip of him'. These people were then 'shown' the errors of their ways after we had all been forced to sprint around the buildings and beasted again and again whilst the offender was forced to watch his platoon suffer for his offence. There were also many fights and beatings after the instructors had left in the evenings. At 5' 2" and weighing only 7 stones I could have easily become a victim, but apart from one occasion, I managed to escape the endless bruising that was inflicted on some. A fat idiot from Salford had taken a dislike to me from day one, he was nearly twice my size and often slagged me off in an attempt at proving his toughness to others, but I generally kept out of his way as much as I could, his insults bouncing off me. One day he came into the room after receiving an instructors tongue lashing for again lagging behind on a run, and asked me what I was looking at. I replied; 'nothing' and tried to bury my head in my locker hoping not to provoke him further, but he swaggered over and continued to verbally push me into a reaction. I was scared of this guy and tried to carry on working on my locker layout, ignoring his shoves and pushes, but he then proceeded to pull all of my kit off the locker shelves onto the floor and kick it across the room. It was only then that I attempted my first head butt which unfortunately missed; a scuffle ensued that was broken up by the other lads. No fighting in the rooms as the highly polished floors would be scuffed. 'FIGHT!' Was shouted and into the customary bare concrete floored drying room we went, with as many of his mates, my mates and anyone else who could squeeze in. They always say that bullies are cowards and if you stand up to them they back down, not this one! This guy proceeded for the next five minutes to beat me to a pulp, needless to say, I didn't win. The next morning on muster parade the sergeant instructor came among us on his routine inspection, looked me over and said; 'Who did that to you lad' (I was black eyed, cut, bruised and sore all over),'I fell over sergeant' I replied, he said, 'well don't fall over anyone bigger than you again!' He stopped at fatty, sporting his minor abrasions and asked him if he fell over as well. I still took some verbal stick from fatty over the next few weeks but he didn't touch me again. He still continued to have trouble keeping up with us on the runs and towards the end of Z Company, a few weeks before we passed out of recruit training in December 1972, I took great pleasure in watching him hand his kit in prior to his discharge. Another one bites the dust, good riddance fatty!

After Christmas leave I returned to camp in early January to begin my next phase of training - back to school! The survivors of Z Company were moved to the top camp company lines. As a future member of the Queens Lancashire Regiment in the

Kings Division, I was posted to the Kings Division Company. We were in the same type of buildings and billeted among the 16-17 year old junior soldiers of the I.J.L.B. (Infantry Junior Leaders Battalion), who were all at various stages of their training. We new boys did our best to keep out of the way of these older lads especially the junior NCOs who were looked upon as gods, wearing the red stripes of their respective junior ranks. Junior Corporals and Sergeants even had their own bunks, or single rooms, and they sure liked to scream at us new lads. For the next year our training as future NCOs of the British Army was a routine of drill, physical fitness and education. Back in the classrooms I had the edge on many of my soldier classmates, my teachers at Arnold School must have got through to me more than I had thought. The year dragged slowly for me though as I watched the lads who were in their last year as juniors going through their military training. I envied them, especially when the Northern Ireland training came around, 'you lads won't be doing this next year,' they'd say, 'it will be all over soon', and at the time I thought it would be. The situation in Northern Ireland had then been going on for four years, and we regularly read the news reports. I really thought back then, that when it would be my turn, it would be over; history has since proved me wrong.

In January 1974, after Christmas leave once more, I arrived back at Park Hall camp for the year I had waited for. I had been in the Army for just under eighteen months and was finally going to learn how to use the rifle I had carried countless times on the drill square. The year 1974 swept by, we were worked and trained hard. The weapons training and range work was near endless, and we became skilled in shooting, cleaning, handling and even instructing on every weapon in the Infantry's arsenal; from pistols to rifles, machine guns, grenades, to the 66mm and 84mm Anti-tank weapons. We became skilled operators on Radios, signals and codes, taught combat medical skills from treating gunshot wounds to major injuries from Artillery, mortars and mines. We spent week upon week in the Welsh mountains and forests learning battle skills, map reading, survival, defensive and offensive tactics, patrolling and camouflage and concealment techniques. That year was non stop and as the year ended, we began to train for one of the Army's major roles - Northern Ireland. All through the year I had been sure that the troubles in Northern Ireland would be over by the time I left training and now, knowing that my battalion 1 QLR was due to go to Northern Ireland for an 18 month tour, I took great interest in our Instructors words. Finally before Christmas after the final passing out parade finished, we were called in the Commanding Officer's office to receive our postings to our regular battalions. I had made it through two and a half years of Junior Leaders and could not wait to join my parent regiment, 1 QLR, but unfortunately for me and my six junior QLR comrades it was not to be. The battalion was going to Northern Ireland next month, but we were told we couldn't join them until we had reached 18 years of age. On March 11th, 1971 three young Scottish soldiers aged 17 and a half had been abducted from a pub and murdered by the IRA, the bodies of the young soldiers were found in Ligoniel, just outside Belfast, and they had all been shot dead. Soldiers now had to be eighteen before serving in Northern Ireland, so I was to be attached to the 1st Battalion of the Royal Irish Rangers until I reached 18, another six months to wait, I was one cheesed off ex- junior soldier!

I left Park Hall Camp for the last time in December 1974. We were the last junior soldiers to leave Park Hall Camp; it was closed down and demolished soon after. We arrived in Warminster, Wiltshire, in January 1975 and as I walked through the gates of 1 RIR, my new home for the next six months, the new role I would be undertaking was as a member of the Infantry demonstration battalion. This meant tearing around Salisbury plain, playing the enemy for the members of various courses that came through Warminster. A very cushy job! I learned several skills whilst with the Irish Rangers, drinking was one of them; pub life at weekends was frenzied for these guys. As a seventeen year old I got into some states and woke up in some funny places, but I managed to stay out of any major military rule breaking, and I even got to meet girls!

In April I was sent to Cyprus for six weeks, attached to 2 Royal Irish Rangers on United Nations duty, as the island had been invaded by Turkish forces a year earlier. I didn't get to see much more than guard posts out in the wilderness during my time in the country, but we got a medal for being there although this took 8 years for me to receive. On my last month I was given a dream opportunity, a two week driving course, on the final test day, I sat nervously in my 3/4 ton Long Wheel Base Land Rover awaiting the test examiner. A jovial Irish Colour Sergeant jumped in and we proceeded on my driving test, 'just foller my directions boy', he said in his thick Irish accent, which thankfully I had now got used to. I was directed out of camp, through Warminster town centre to a supermarket where his wife met us and piled their shopping into the rear of the vehicle and climbed in. I then took her back to their home on the married quarters estate, helped to unload the shopping, drove back to camp and told; 'well done boy dat's a pass!' Two weeks later I left Warminster with a travel warrant for Liverpool docks where I would link up with a ferry to Belfast on the 8th July. The ferry docked in Belfast at 6am the following morning on the 9th July 1975, my 18th Birthday.

2.

Thankfully due to all the fitness training and possibly the three meals a day supplied by Her Majesty's government over the last three years, I had put on four stones in weight and grown another ten inches. Gone was the 5'2", 7 stone, fifteen year old boy. I stepped off the ferry that morning thinking I was a man going proudly off to war, though when I think back on it I was still a boy, but felt indestructible. I was collected at the docks by a 'Q' van, a civilian vehicle driven by soldiers wearing civilian clothes. We left Belfast docks, drove out through the city and headed south into County Down and arrived at my battalion barracks at Ballykinler. I was to become a new member of 2 platoon, A Company, 1 QLR. The battalion was now six months into the eighteen month tour as province reserve battalion, which meant we could find ourselves moving to any part of Northern Ireland to assist any Regiment who may require additional support and troops in their tactical areas. For me though, before I could work with my new platoon I had to attend a week long 'Northern Ireland Reinforcement Training Team' course. The course gave you instruction in up to date patrolling skills, the specialised equipment and weapons used in Northern Ireland, along with the 'Yellow Card' instruction of shooting when fired upon or attacked. This yellow card was carried by all soldiers, and was supposed to protect a soldier who may be forced into firing his weapon at any terrorist who he may come across, from any criminal proceedings that may follow. Many servicemen, however, considered this card to be a hindrance more than a help, if you followed the rules of engagement to the letter you would certainly not face criminal charges but you would probably not get the terrorist either. The course culminated in us being sent out on patrol with units serving in Belfast, to get an idea of life on the streets. I was sent to the Springfield road area of Belfast, a mainly Catholic, Nationalist area, where the IRA were very active in their attacks on the Army and Police. My first patrol was to be a memorable one.

I was the fourth man of a brick (four man) patrol, along with three members of the Royal Highland Fusiliers Regiment who were on a four month tour of duty in that area. As I was the new boy they only gave me 10 rounds for my rifle, I remember the big double gates opening as we dashed out of the camp on a zigzag run, this was to make it hard for you to be hit by an IRA sniper who may be waiting in the area to shoot, and where better than outside a camp. We sprinted out of the gates for 30-40 yards and settled down into patrol formation, I was the rear, right hand man. I had not been on the street for more than ten seconds of my first patrol when BANG! BANG! BANG! BANG! BANG! A burst of automatic fire hurtled in our direction - I couldn't believe it! As I dashed forward and took cover behind a concrete filled oil drum, in a line of other oil drums designed to keep cars loaded with explosives away from the camp perimeter, it crossed my mind that this may be another training test. The brick commander gave a contact report over the radio (contact made with enemy), while we watched the area further up the street from where the shots had come from, I looked back towards the camp gates only fifty yards away as more soldiers came out to assist us with the follow-up procedures. I honestly didn't know what was going on. It was later discovered that a car was parked on the top of the road from the camp, and as we came out of the gates, the car moved off and turned left, and as it did someone fired a Thompson submachine gun at us through the rear passenger window. A bit of a cowboy attack was the feeling among those that knew, although I didn't, all I knew was that I had been here on the streets for less than ten seconds, I had a year to go and I had been shot at! How was I going to make it through the year? Amazingly, to me anyway, we carried on with the patrol after more troops had been dispersed to follow up on our 'shooting', two hours later I made it back through the gates alive and well. That evening I was tasked to return out on a mobile (vehicle born) patrol; two Land Rovers stripped down to bare essentials minus doors, windscreen and canvas cover sped through the gates without any surprises this time. One of the tasks we had been given was to inform a mother that her seventeen year old son had been found kneecapped an hour earlier by another army patrol, The two Land Rovers moved into the victims street and we debussed the vehicles and moved along the street on foot until we came to the mothers front door, I was covering the patrol commander as he knocked and awaited the answer. The mother came to the door, and the patrol commander passed on the details, the mother casually said; 'right! I'll see him tomorrow', and closed the door in the commanders face. I had only been in Northern Ireland for one day and was already learning of the harsh reality of the situation here. With the NIRRT course now over I returned to my battalion and rejoined 2 platoon, a more enlightened but still young soldier. For the next year we would be regularly called out to trouble spots and flare-ups in various parts of the province; Armagh, Portadown, Newry, Lisburn and Belfast. On one occasion the whole of A Company was sent to the Tiger Bay area of Belfast to assist the unit there, A Company were put onto one street to patrol for 24 hours, a whole company of over 100 men walking up and down one street for 24 hours to show a presence. One funny reminder though was at about 2am I was stood with my section getting a brew from the back of one of the Saracen armoured cars, when a bloke came ambling out of his front door with a fully grown, toothless Lion on a chain and casually walked past us as he took it out for its walk. No-one said anything to him as he toddled off and returned from his walk, he didn't speak to us and the Lion just looked at us as we smelt it pass us. Strange place this! My favourite 'hot spot' though was Portadown, every time we were sent there we somehow managed to get involved in riots, shootings, bombings or a mixture of all of them. My best time was being sent to Portadown with 1 platoon as the platoon commander's driver, the platoon commander was a lieutenant nicknamed 'Sooty' and was a bit of a legend - Sooty could fuck anything up. He had a big, stupid Irish wolfhound called 'Ulf' who enjoyed crapping in strange places, including on the centre seat of the Land Rover on the drive from Ballykinler to Portadown. I was driving and Sooty was in the passenger seat, Sooty just looked over the dogs head at me as though I'd done it, while Ulf proudly sat in it throughout the two hour drive, and I had the pleasure of cleaning it up later. He once took us out on a foot patrol and came across a sewer drain that looked to him as though it had been moved recently, so he stuck his rifle barrel into the drain to lever it open, it didn't budge, and when he withdrew his barrel it had bent to nearly forty five degrees, so he had to carry out the rest of the patrol with his bent rifle barrel as the rest of us just giggled at him when he wasn't looking – at least he was good for morale! Another very memorable occasion for me was during one of the riots we attended in the infamous Obins Street of Portadown, I managed to use the Federal Riot Gun (FRG) that fired large plastic bullets, called baton rounds. I got to fire a few rounds into the crowd of rioters as they pelted us with bricks and bottles. My best shot ever with this weapon was when one particular irritatingly mouthy rioter ran out from the crowd and was about to launch a brick in our direction. I aimed and fired the baton gun, the baton round hit him hard and square in the right shoulder spinning him round so fast, he fell flat on the floor face first. He didn't half squeal! Even better to come was a minute later as he struggled to get to his feet, my mate 'Big S' hit him with another round square in the back - it still makes me smile. Minutes later the IRA dispersed the rioting crowd for us, as we stood behind the shields taking a hail of bricks and bottles, two unseen gunmen came out from behind the crowd and fired several shots over their heads in our general direction, none of our guys were hit nor came close, but in front of us, the rioting crowd panicked. The heroic brick throwers hit the deck in panic, unsure of where the shots had come from, and the rioters began getting to their feet and moving into the cover of doorways and side streets. The fun of stoning British soldiers no longer appealed to them if they were going to get shot from behind! A few hardy idiots threw the odd brick, but always wary of what was going on behind them, maybe they didn't have much faith in their comrades marksmanship. The IRA quickly killed off the faith of the rioters and twenty minutes later the streets were back under control, albeit with debris and glass left all over the road. I actually enjoyed the days of the rioting, we could often give some back in return. To be honest though, the majority of the time spent in Northern Ireland during that tour, was a dull life of routine patrolling and manning vehicle checkpoints broken up by occasional bursts of excitement. The following July we left Ballykinler for our new home at Chester.

During the years of 1975 and 1976, whilst I was in Northern Ireland, 28 soldiers were killed and 393 injured, over 300 civilians died and more than 1500 injured due to terrorist actions. I don't remember being scared during that tour, my motto was; 'it won't happen to me'. In fact, except for one sad loss the battalion was very lucky. Our fatality was killed when a Saracen turned over in Armagh, crushing him to death, a tragic accident not forgotten by his friends, but the bigger picture was the battalion on the whole had been lucky despite being sent to all the serious trouble spots in those eighteen months of the tour. For me though, I'd just completed my first tour of Northern Ireland!

3.

In July of 1976 we came back from leave to our new home at Saighton camp, Chester, which was an old camp that consisted of the wooden spider blocks similar to the buildings of my junior soldier days. Chester itself was a good posting as it wasn't far from our homes in Lancashire, full of good pubs and plenty of local females. The downside to it was that whilst in Chester, we weren't just soldiers, during the many national strikes of that year we got our turns at being firemen when they were out, and stood in as dustbin men when they too were out on strike, needless to say, we didn't think much of civvies at that time. In January 1977 we were sent on a month's jungle training in the Gambia, West Africa, living in a tented camp carved out of the jungle deep in the country. Coming from England in a chilly January to the searing heat of Africa took some adjusting to as did the change in wildlife, when working alongside the river Gambia in the mangrove swamps, I always felt that the many crocodiles were too close and the leeches much closer, I once found seven leeches on one leg after a wet and muddy patrol. Our toilet facilities in the jungle camp was an eight foot deep pit over which was positioned the 'thunder box' as it was called, the thunder box was a large ten man toilet. If you can imagine a large wooden frame roughly twelve foot by six foot and on top of this frame were ten deposit holes leading into the pit, this you merrily sat upon, back to back and side by side with your buddies happily dumping next to you, while clutching your toilet paper in one hand, in the other insect repellent in case of attack as the ants bit and hurt! Towards the end of each week the toilet on the edge of the camp had to be cleaned by dousing the waste pit in diesel and burning it. It was then covered in a chemical ready for the next batch of white bottoms. One week when the thunder box was pulled away from the pit, a nice fat surprise awaited us. In the bottom of the pit and writhing around in the crap and new found sunlight was a 30 foot long python, which had somehow come out of the jungle probably at night, and entered the pit via one of the toilet seats on the thunder box. The Royal Engineers attached to us, managed to kill and drag it out on display before it was skinned for someone's souvenir, I still shudder to think how many times I may have sat on that thunder box with my white dangly bits hanging down while that huge snake lay in the bottom watching me dump and eating the crap, I hate snakes - and that was one big snake!

Back in Chester, and our jungle holiday over, we were told to begin training again for Northern Ireland, we had been given a four month tour of duty in South Armagh - nicknamed 'bandit country', from August to December of 1977. A Company, my company had got the town of Crossmaglen, arguably the worst and most dangerous posting in Northern Ireland. This time I knew it was going to be a tough tour and I was already apprehensive. We were told straight out to expect some casualties and even deaths among us on this tour; this was not going to be a holiday. We left Liverpool docks for Belfast on the Royal Fleet Auxiliary ship, Sir Galahad (later to be sunk during the Falklands War), on the 5th August 1977. I remember silently thinking as we left the dock, would I be coming back this time? The Crossmaglen base consisted of two mortar proof submarine type buildings, and wooden shower blocks, some wooden sleeping blocks for the unfortunates should we be mortared, and the police building. It was small and confined, but for the next four months we would be out on patrol more than we would be inside the base. The three platoons of A Company would rotate; two days on rural patrolling then two days on town patrolling and two days on camp guard duty. It was all go and non stop work, and was beginning to think you could meet yourself coming off patrol as you went out again. It was a hard tour and we did indeed take casualties though I didn't know then that I was going to be on the patrol that was to get the worst of it. Crossmaglen base was like a mini fortress. There were five watchtower type sangars overlooking the base perimeter with the helipad at the rear of the base, Helicopters being the only means of transport and resupply. The roads were considered too dangerous for military vehicles to travel on, with the threat from mines, ambush and culvert bombs. The only other mode of travel and the best used was by foot. Just up the road from the base some thirty yards away was Baruki Sanger, the main two man watchtower that overlooked Crossmaglen market square. Baruki Sanger was named after Robert Baruki a member of the Parachute regiment who was killed on that spot by a bicycle bomb. A bicycle simply left against the wall, but with the frame packed with explosives and someone ready to press a button as a soldier walks by - deadly! I was out by Baruki Sanger early one morning, when I was called back into the base. I was told the other half of our platoon was tasked for a rural patrol out to Cullaville on the Southern Irish border. I had to replace Woody who had twisted his ankle so he was to do my town patrol and I got his rural patrol, call sign 12 Lima was to be a twelve man multiple patrol of three (four man) bricks, call signs 12 Lima, 12 Delta and 12 Foxtrot. The command brick Lima was to be made up of Sergeant Sid, the patrol commander and three volunteers of HQ platoon. Among them my mate Pete, the company store man, Copper the company medic and JS the company clerk. I had been 'volunteered' to take Woody's place as radio operator in 12 Delta. Steph a Lance Corporal in command of Delta was an old and good friend of mine from my junior soldier days. Tet's and Radar were also mates and that made up our brick. Foxtrot was made up of another Lance Corporal Joey K, with Eric, Kev and Knipey, all friends so I was not too upset about the changeover. We were told prior to our departure by Sid, the overall patrol commander that shots had been heard in the Cullaville area during the night and we were to patrol the area and if possible question the locals on the shootings, it sounded easy enough. We left the base via the back gates and set off on foot across country towards the small village of Cullaville just over two miles to the west of Crossmaglen and surrounded on three sides by the Southern Irish border. The patrol down there was routine, but as we approached the village the atmosphere had changed. As we entered the outskirts of Cullaville, we could see an apparently abandoned car, an old Rover with its boot half open left on the cross roads that the village was centered on. There were also no people about, it felt definitely wrong, and we knew it, but we also had a job to do. Sid moved his brick (Lima) closer into the village to check the number plates of the vehicle. The two other bricks covered the border areas that overlooked the village. I turned to Steph and said 'any minute now', to which he replied; 'I'll start the countdown!' Sid moved his brick closer to the car and put Copper and JS into fire positions observing down the roads and moved to the opposite side of the road with Pete who had Limas radio with the intention of sending the plate check. Sid was just taking the radio handset from Pete when BOOM! A radio controlled bomb detonated only feet from them. Pete had been facing in the direction of the bomb and took the full force of it. The blast forced him backwards into Sid and knocked him clear into the centre of the road, I watched in disbelief at the unreality of what had just happened, then dived for cover as I realised the debris from the explosion was beginning to fall around us. Some 'brave' IRA volunteer had sat behind a hedgerow somewhere, probably across the border in safety and pressed his little button to detonate the bomb. Once the debris had landed, Steph set off like a gazelle leaping over garden fences to get to the wounded. I got on our radio and gave a 'contact' report informing them of our whereabouts and telling them we had taken casualties then went to help with the wounded. The whole of the Lima brick had been hit by the explosion. Copper and JS were not too bad, they had been caught by the blast but had no injuries, though they were both in shock. Pete and Sid were not good at all, Pete had taken the full force head on, his face was a bloody and a tattered mess, it was clear he had serious head injuries. Sid had been blown across the road and hit on top of the head by a large rock thrown from the explosion, he was struggling to talk and give out orders. I helped Sid to the side of the road and into cover along with Tets, and tried to calm him down. He was bleeding badly from his head and we applied a field dressing to stop the blood flow. Sid our patrol commander was out of it, meanwhile Steph and Knipey had got to Pete who was in an even worse condition. They picked him up and he managed to stagger to his feet, aided by Steph and Knipey he managed to cross the road to cover at the front of a house. Steph kicked open the door and they placed Pete on the floor in the hallway. Copper was still in shock, but as company medic went to assist in giving Pete first aid. Pete's injuries were bad, his head was a mass of blood and flesh, and from one look it was obvious he had lost an eye. He needed more than first aid and fast. The now angry homeowner had come out from behind her curtains and into the hallway to demand an explanation of this Army invasion of her property. She was a middle aged woman and on looking at Pete's injuries coldly yelled 'don't let him bleed on my carpet!' Steph told the cow in no uncertain terms, to 'Fuck off!' I was finding it hard to contact our base to update them on our situation. The handset and mike were playing up, and had to use Pete's as spares. I eventually got hold of our base by speaking through Pete's' microphone that was coated in blood and tissue, they informed me that help and the airborne medivac was on its way.

We found out later that RAF Puma helicopters based at Bessbrook were not eager to come out because of poor weather conditions. As fortune would have it; a passing Royal Navy Wessex helicopter heard our plight and offered to assist. This was gratefully accepted; Navy pilots serving in Northern Ireland were always the much respected by us ground troops. Soon, other reinforcements began to arrive. First on the scene our own O.C. Major P and Stewart the S.A.S. liaison officer based at Crossmaglen, they had got an RUC police sergeant to drive

Me in Crossmaglen, 1977.

them down in his own car. Then an army gazelle helicopter landed and dropped four Quick Reaction Force troops onto the ground. The military machine began to swing into action as more troops arrived by chopper. Pete and Sid were immediately evacuated, soon followed by Copper and J.S. Throughout the day, the area was secured so that the A.T.O.

(Ammunition Technician Officer) team who worked as bomb disposal and clearance could gather evidence and forensics from the scene. One flight came in with some huge yard brushes, we then got the job to sweep and clear the rubble from the roads so they could be re-opened once the area had been cleared. The troops began to disperse, being flown back to their various locations, finally the last troops to leave Cullaville that day were the eight of us left of the patrol. No helicopter for us, we walked back to Crossmaglen. Back at the base we were informed that Copper and J.S. would soon be back with us. Sid would take a bit longer to recover but would be O.K. Pete was undergoing surgery, his wounds more serious.

Pete was later invalided out of the Army; he lost his eyesight that day and would be blind for life. I am still in touch with Pete; he now lives in the south of England near to an ex-serviceman's home for the blind. He has remarkably retained his sense of humour, I rang him once and he answered the phone saying, 'if this is not a stunningly beautiful woman, I'm hanging up.' I wonder to myself whether I could have coped with those injuries he had sustained. A very brave and courageous man is Peter. The IRA took his eyesight that day but not his spirit.

Crossmaglen was a hard town, soldiers were not welcome at all, although I don't believe the people there hated us as much as they made out. Fear of IRA reprisals would always be on their minds. As we patrolled the streets we would not be spoken to or even looked at unless we stopped them for security checks. That was except for one polite old man. He was in his sixties, I believe he was an ex-serviceman and had been in the Second World War; he lived at home and cared for his house-bound sick wife. In the mornings he would walk into the town square to do his errands and shopping then go back home to care for his wife. If he passed a patrol, he would casually say 'Morning' or 'Hello boys' and walk by, a harmless, polite and proud man, until one night, when four masked IRA gunmen came to visit. He was forced from his home at gunpoint in front of his sick wife, taken to a field close to the border, kicked to the ground then shot twice in the back of his head with an Armalite rifle. His crime? Saying 'Morning boys', the official IRA statement was that an 'informer' had been executed. I was on the operation to recover the mans body from the field. As it was feared the body may have been booby-trapped, he lay in the field for two days and nights until the area and his body was cleared. An early Christmas present for us, would have been to have bumped into these gunmen, but they would have gone back across the border long ago. It is with little wonder that the people of Crossmaglen are scared.

Shortly before our tour ended, in December 1977, a derelict building about a mile from Crossmaglen was found to contain hidden two way radio equipment and other items belonging to the IRA. It was decided that this derelict building should be kept under surveillance, in the hope that somebody may arrive to collect the equipment. I was 'volunteered' to take part in this operation. Again eight men were picked from the company, to occupy two, four man observation posts that were placed around the buildings, in hedgerows and bushes in the area. We were to stay in the locations for up to four days. After that time we would be replaced by fresh troops. We moved into our positions shortly after dark, that first night of the operation it snowed heavily, and by first light we lay under, or in, three feet of snow. For four days and nights we lay in these positions, we ate, drank, slept, watched, urinated and shat in our positions. The snow covered and concealed us but also allowed no movement from our positions. By the end of those four days we were very cold, very wet, miserable and tired. The relief troops from the battalion Close Observation platoon moved into our positions shortly before dawn on the fourth morning. And it was just our luck that 45 minutes after the relief had taken over from our positions; two IRA men arrived to collect the radio equipment. As these men entered the

South Armagh 1977

A Company 1ˢᵗ Bn Queens Lancashire Regt, Crossmaglen 1977

building they were challenged by the Close Observation platoon, faced by highly trained and armed British soldiers, they immediately surrendered and were arrested. A success story for the battalion as both men were high on the wanted list.

The tour ended on the 9th December 1977. We were going home for Christmas, to be followed by a posting to Cyprus in January. The unit replacing us was the second battalion of the Royal Green Jackets (2RGJ). A claim to fame I have, is that among those soldiers replacing us in Crossmaglen, was the young eighteen year old private Andy McNab later to become a famous S.A.S. soldier and author of Bravo Two Zero!

4.

We arrived on the sunshine island of Cyprus in late January 1978. We were based at Episkopi Garrison on the island for just over two years. It was not all sun, sea, sand and booze; we had some work to do as well. The three rifle companies of the battalion would rotate on a month of training exercises, one month at Ayious Nikolaous, guarding and patrolling the signals regiment base at the East of the island, and one month of Quick Reaction Deployment which provided the British base areas' security and the security of the Joint RAF and the signals detachment on Mount Troodos.

We had barely settled into our duties on Cyprus when, whilst on the Quick Reaction Deployment role, 2 platoon received an order to 'stand to' - immediate readiness to move. We quickly assembled our gear and arrived into the briefing room. A civilian passenger aircraft had been hi-jacked and was en-route to Cyprus. The plane landed at Larnaca airport later that day.

Larnaca was not under British jurisdiction, so the security aspects fell onto the Cypriot authorities to deal with, however, British assistance had been offered and we were to remain on immediate notice to move. S.A.S. units in the U.K were also alerted. The Egyptian airliner now on the ground at Larnaca airport was under control of German terrorists, the passengers and crew aboard the aircraft were being held hostage. Heavy negotiations were being held with the terrorists for the release of the hostages, though unbeknown to us, was the fact that Egypt was in the process of planning its own rescue operation. On the night of the 19th February 1978, the hijacked airliner stood on the airfield perimeter, searchlights covered the area of the plane. Greek Cypriot national guardsmen had surrounded the aircraft as well as the airport itself. The remainder of the airport was in darkness including the runways. An Egyptian Hercules transport plane landed on the runway and began to disperse Egyptian commandos to assault the hijacked aircraft. Then all chaos was let loose! Whether the Egyptian government had taken it upon themselves to instigate a rescue operation or they had permission that had somehow not been relayed to the Greek Cypriot National Guard, I don't know. As the Egyptian commandos moved towards the hijacked aircraft they clashed with the Greek National Guard and one hell of a fire fight followed with the Egyptians coming off worst. The Egyptian Hercules aircraft was destroyed on the ground, and the Egyptian commandos without cover and caught on the open ground of the airstrip took many casualties, they were forced to surrender. Our platoon received its notice to move to assist the repatriation of the Egyptians. The badly wounded were handed over to the Cypriots for medical attention and the Egyptian survivors and the dead loaded onto trucks and a coach and handed over to the control of British forces, us, to be immediately repatriated to Egypt. We escorted the Egyptians to R.A.F. Akrotiri to await a second Egyptian Hercules to land and collect them. As we waited for their aircraft I chatted in broken English to the commandos and offered them cigarettes. We all felt sympathy for these guys; they had come here to rescue the hostages and ended up being fired upon by supposed friendly troops. They were big guys these Egyptian commandos, though unfortunately on a bare runway without cover they made big targets. They left R.A.F. Akrotiri taking their dead with them. The one good thing to come out of it was, during the melee the terrorists aboard the hijacked aircraft thought the shooting was a prelim to an assault on the aircraft and negotiated surrender. The hostages at least were happy.

Cyprus did have plenty of sun, sea, sand and even more booze. As there were very few approachable females on the island many of the lads hit the booze, and it wasn't long before the battalion got itself a bad name as Infantry regiments do. I even overheard some R.A.F. wives gossiping about the battalion, one said; 'These QLRs have just come here from Northern Ireland' to which one replied, 'it sounds like the best place to send them back to! 'To be fair there were a lot of recreational activities to take up but without the female attraction, the lads soon attacked the cheap island booze, at least the ugly women looked better after a few. For many of the lads it was going to be a long two years.

I wasn't one of those who wasted all his time in the Cypriot bars and clubs. I got a duty free car, I did a sub-aqua diving course and joined the sub-aqua and snorkeling club in Akrotiri bay. I also did a parachute course, but after my first three jumps I went sick with a badly bruised backside, the medic on duty there gave me some form of Algipan and pain relievers. He even offered to rub the cream onto my poorly bum cheeks for me; I declined his offer and thought it would be better if I did it! I painfully learned to land better, to complete my course.

Whilst on the tour on Cyprus we took part in a joint Navy/Army exercise. H.M.S. Bulwark arrived on the island and we embarked on it for a two week exercise of hostage rescue, and air and sea assault landings. H.M.S. Bulwark was a helicopter carrier used mainly by the marines. For those two weeks we lived on board ship and began practising heli-borne assaults and rescues on land. I didn't know at the time that one sailor on board was a John Rowley from Stoke-on-Trent, who I was to cross paths with some years later in far different circumstances.

In the March of 1980 our tour of the holiday island ended and we returned to the U.K. Our new home was at Tern Hill camp in Market Drayton, Shropshire. Before I would get there I would have to drive my duty free car, a mini clubman back to England. It took me and my mate Jack nine days to get back with a few planned detours; it was a trouble free trip until we arrived on the London south circular road where for some reason it took us seven hours to get round London. Traffic was horrendous, we heard later on the car radio that the day I had chosen to arrive back in London, was the day the Libyan Embassy was taken over by Arab terrorists. The rest is S.A.S. history!

After leave we settled into Market Drayton. One of our first bits of news was that the battalion had been tipped for another tour of Northern Ireland from October 1980 through to March 81. It was soon to be back to South Armagh for us, perhaps somebody else had overheard the R.A.F. wives conversation other than me back in Cyprus. So it was back into Northern Ireland training; A company were going to Newry this time, C Company to Crossmaglen. We arrived back in Northern Ireland on 23rd October 1980; it was to be my third tour. The main difference for me personally was that I was now a Corporal, and a section commander, responsible for one Lance Corporal and seven soldiers.

The Northern Ireland of the eighties for the Army was a far less dangerous place than when I first arrived here. The police were now back on the streets and no longer required the Army to assist them in much of their duties. The tour for me was one of routine patrolling, dull vehicle checks and guard duties. I was getting bored. The battalion returned this time intact on 12th March 1981. After leave it was back to Market Drayton. My Army career ended one year later, March 1982. I had served nine years and 162 days. I was all fired up and ready to rejoin one month later when the Falklands erupted, but was not to be, as 1 QLR did not play a part in the war. It was Civvy Street for me.

5.

After leaving the Army, I made a living truck driving. I passed my HGV 1 course and for the next ten years I found myself enjoying the life of a civilian and driving articulated trucks in and around Europe. It was and still is a life to which I was suited.

In the early months of 1992 I heard the news and watched the outbreak of the civil war in Yugoslavia on TV. Like many others I did not fully understand the situation over there, until I watched the 'Inside Story' TV documentary entitled 'Dogs of War'. It was about British ex-soldiers fighting for Croatia in the civil war. I became fascinated by the situation there and took more and more interest in the news reports coming out of Yugoslavia. I began to see the Croatian and Bosnian fight against the Serbian dominated Yugoslavian National Army (JNA) as a one sided affair. A former communist army was attacking the land and people of Croatia and Bosnia because they had demanded independence from the Serbians and its communist regime. Croatia and Bosnia had become too westernized and had angered their communist 'masters'. Independence was denied and Serbia had invaded first Croatia then Bosnia, I began to feel drawn to the war. I began to have the idea of going out there myself to join the fight. I admit that while I had mentally sided with the Croat and Bosnian alliance, another thing in my mind was that, during my Army days and the training that had gone with it, I had never experienced real war, although I had seen action in Northern Ireland I would still ask myself would 'what would I have been really like in a real war situation?' And 'how would I have reacted in real battle?' What is it really like, terrifying or exciting? I wanted to know - I knew then that I had made the decision to join the war! It was Saturday 21st June 1992. The following day I was due to go out in a truck bound for Germany. I had a second driver coming with me, a friend of mine called 'Paddy'. I packed a

Bergen and set off to work as usual and I told only Paddy of my plan, which was to complete the German trip and once the truck was loaded up for the return to the U.K. I would leave it with Paddy to drive back, and set off by myself south towards Yugoslavia by train.

Two days later the truck was loaded in Monchengladbach in Germany. I got Paddy to drop me off at the train station and we parted company, I got a train that afternoon to Munich and arrived around 11 pm. There was a train bound for Zagreb, Croatia the next afternoon. I tried to get some sleep on the station that night, but I was continually awoken by police checking passports. I eventually gave up by 5.30am and had a wash and shave, then bought my train ticket for Zagreb. The train was to leave at 1300 hours from platform 13, I wasn't superstitious but I hoped that wasn't a warning. It was still early and the English newspapers had not arrived so I bought the previous days Daily Star dated 23rd June. My star sign said - believe it or not - 'You have made a decision and now must have the courage to go through with it'! I caught the train for Zagreb, travelling via Villach (Austria), and an hour later I had crossed the Yugoslav (Slovenian) border, we passed a train of fifteen double-decker car transporter carriages with cars on both decks, the whole lot had been burnt out, by who or what I don't know. There were lots of Slovenian flags flying from buildings and roadsides as the train passes through, but all the people seem to be just going about their business.

I entered Croatia via Medova and arrived in Zagreb around 10.00pm. I didn't fancy spending the night on this station so I hoisted my Bergen and decided to make for one of the two campsites marked on the map, my first big mistake! After a stupid map reading error, to which I set off in the wrong direction, I finally made the first site around midnight only to find it had been taken over by the police who were using it as a transit camp. I got out the map and set off for the second one only to find that this was now a student complex. It was now 2.00am, I had walked with my Bergen on my back for about eight or nine miles and I was knackered, so I unrolled my sleeping bag by a hedgerow on a large traffic island and fell asleep.

I woke up at 7.00am, and after a quick double check that I had not missed the campsite I set off back towards the train station and a rethink. On my return I sat around on the station watching soldiers getting onto trains returning to their units and others coming back home, it reminded me of world war two newsreel films I had seen. I hadn't much money so I needed a plan as well as food and a good night's kip. That night I had to sleep out again, this time I got a taxi to drop me off at another campsite marked on the map, ten miles outside Zagreb, the cab cost me a tenner, probably two quid if I had been a local. The campsite was in the grounds of a motel and deserted. When I went in to pay for the site (30p), they offered me the motel facilities. I grabbed a bath and then I put up a basha (tent), unrolled my sleeping bag and crawled in. I woke at 8:00am, made a brew, scoffed a tin of London grill, packed up and set off on foot back towards Zagreb. As I walked back along the bank of the river Sava, a camouflaged painted Second World War type biplane flew overhead, obviously Croatian; I believe the Serbs have MIG's. I got back to Zagreb three hours later, I had walked the ten miles from the campsite, and I felt pretty good; it must be down to the sleep and breakfast. I spent the rest of the day, hanging around the train station and got a ticket to Osijek, the last known report I had of the international brigade mentioned in the documentary I had watched back in the UK, the ticket cost me 550 dinars (£2), my next problem was that the train did not leave until the next night! As I sat on the platform that evening wasting time, a trainload of returning troops came in, as they were getting off I noticed one of them was not only carrying a loaded AK47 assault rifle, as they all were, but this one had slung from his hip a pistol and over his back a 64mm Anti-tank launcher (Warsaw pact version of our own 66mm light anti-tank weapon), just as I was thinking he has got something to show his mum, I heard a metallic thud. As his mate walked alongside him he accidentally kicked the object 'Rambo' had dropped - a live hand-grenade! I remember my eyes focusing on the pin as it rolled along the platform, thankfully, even though I had already decided where I was going head first, the pin stayed in and he picked it up from the now silent platform, stuck it into his webbing pouch and walked on with a red face - that blew his posing!

I had another rough night sleeping between two hamburger stands, this time I was not alone, as the station at night becomes a sleeping area for refugees and the homeless. It was another long day spent in and around this rundown station as I waited for the 23:40pm train for Osijek. The town was supposed to be surrounded on three sides by the Serbian JNA forces, and was the Croatian front line in the eastern sector after the fall of Vukovar. At least with all the walking I had done lately carrying my Bergen, I was a bit fitter for any ducking and diving that may be required. I arrived in Osijek the following morning at 5:05am, now in the front line area and the last known position of the Croatian international brigade including the British company. I got a taxi to where they were rumoured to be housed, but on my arrival I found only a Spanish speaking company, I asked the guard sergeant if he knew of the British company's whereabouts, but he said they had been disbanded and sent home. Not one to give up that easily I went to Osijek's hospital, as I also had got a name of an Englishman who was supposedly recovering from his wounds there. On my arrival at the hospital I was told they had no records of him there at all. A friendly Croatian hospital orderly phoned around for me for over an hour, but finally I was again informed that the English speaking company of the international brigade no longer existed, I had drawn a blank and come over 1200 miles to join a unit that no longer existed. I spent the next hour walking around Osijek taking some photographs, including one of an aircraft undercarriage and a blown bridge over the river Drava. This little town has taken a hammering. Later as I sat waiting for the 11:00am train back to Zagreb and home, I heard someone ask if I spoke English, this was how I met Dick, soon to be nicknamed 'Broadmoor'. He was from Accrington and we had both unknowingly arrived from Zagreb on the same train and were both here for the same purpose. Broadmoor had got the same result as me, except that he had spoken to an English or Welshman called Frenchie who was now in the Croatian army. Frenchie used to be in the British company and had been on the Inside Story documentary about the British soldiers working in Croatia. Frenchie had confirmed that the International Brigade had been disbanded a month ago. We both caught the 11:00am train back to Zagreb. Broadmoor decided he was going to try to join the Croatian army in Zagreb but I didn't fancy the idea. I'd feel better working with other English speaking people. Back in Zagreb I bought an open train ticket home, Broadmoor was waiting for me and I bought him a few beers and a sandwich, he was broke, which I would find out over the years was his usual state.

Osijek

Over the drinks I decided I would catch the evening train home tomorrow so that I could go with Broadmoor for his interview in the morning at the Croatian Army HQ. The next morning, after another bad night on the station, Broadmoor and I made our way to the Croatian HQ in Zagreb. On our arrival we spoke to Tommy, an English speaking journalist who worked for a Croatian forces magazine. It was the start of an unusual day for us both. Earlier on I had told Broadmoor that if he got in then I would also give it a try, if it felt right.

After several hours of waiting and delayed meetings we were finally introduced by Tommy to an officer dressed in civilian clothes who took us to an adjacent, unmarked but very secure building. We were interviewed about our military experience; Broadmoor had served in the French Foreign Legion. The general seemed quite pleased with our military histories and we were both accepted into the Croatian Army. We were to join an HVO unit in Bosnia Herzegovina as soon as transport, weapons and uniforms could be arranged, but tonight we were to spend the night at a commandeered hotel in the mountains North of Zagreb. Later that evening we were driven to the hotel, high up in the mountains in an area called Slijeme. On our arrival at the hotel, Broadmoor and I found that we were the only guests in what looked like a special forces training camp or a jump off point for illicit activities into Bosnia. After being shown to our rooms I had a good shower and washed all of my kit, then went for a meal and a couple of drinks in the bar. Later I had my first nights sleep in a real bed since leaving home. I realised I had just been recruited to fight in the Yugoslavian civil war for Croatia.

The next morning I got up at 6:00am, showered and repacked my kit in case we are moved today. Broadmoor and I spent the morning on the assault course in the woods. I was not as fit as I thought I was and expected to be stiff the next day. In the afternoon we were told we would stay at least one more night and would move out, maybe tomorrow. We also found out we were not the first Brits to have passed through here, some had already come and gone into Bosnia Herzegovina. I watched the TV news that evening – President Mitterrand had visited Sarajevo - there were also scenes of a busload of civilians, 43 in all who had been massacred by the Chetniks (Serbian Militia). The next day was the first of July, I got up early again just to wake up and shout 'White Rabbits' to Broadmoor, who didn't see the funny side, he had got a hangover that morning. Tony, an Australian Croatian working there told us we were to be picked up that night prior to our move to Bosnia; we spent the day walking round the hotel and grounds and left the assault course alone. That evening 'Happy', our newly nicknamed driver, took us down the mountain into Zagreb; we drove through dark back streets until we arrived outside a building at Ogulinska Ulica, another shady looking place. We were dropped off there and we were informed this was 'Club Brcko'. This was the main supply and recruiting office for the area we are going to be working in. The only problem was that they were not expecting us - a communications cock up! In the house was another English guy from Welwyn Garden City called Tom. There was also a Czechoslovakian called Radek, who were both going with us when we leave. Tom is another ex-Legionnaire and Radek has done his National Service in Czechoslovakia. Again nothing had been organized and we were all to stop the night at a flat that Tom and Radek had been using several miles away. We were to return tomorrow when we may get more information. Once at the house, a bar was spotted just up the road, it was Broadmoors idea to use it and he immediately set about scrounging beers for us from the locals, he seems quite good at it. Tom asked if Broadmoor attracted bullets like he does beers! Tom had come here to join a friend of his called Dave who was already working in the Brcko area. Broadmoor was up and away early next morning, and was back in the bar at 8:00am. We were supposed to be picked up at 9:00am but the transport didn't show until after midday when it finally arrived and we were shuttled back to 'Club Brcko'. We were told that we would leave for Bosnia that night and that the area of Brcko in which we are to work is behind Chetnik lines, by 8:00pm things did not look good, the office seemed to run on confusion and us not speaking Croatian didn't help, we seemed to be ignored and not given any information. Although we had been issued a uniform - well, a pair of camouflage trousers, no jackets, boots, weapons or other equipment, though we were told we would get more kit in Zupanja, a village on the Croatian/Bosnian border. Finally, at 11:00pm we were told that we were now not going tonight and those now famous words were used again - maybe tomorrow! Broadmoor had got himself pissed by now and we got him in the van for our lift back to the flat before he upset the people in the office too much. Back at the flat Broadmoor staggered off to the bar again to sell 1000 cigarettes he had nicked from the back of the van. The other two and I have decided to get our heads down and leave Broadmoor to it. I was on the floor again tonight,

Broadmoor slept in the kitchen last night, Tom and Radek share a double bed.

I slept in until 9:30, and then I had to wake up Broadmoor, who looked rough after his all day session yesterday. We returned to the bar at 11:00am, the nine o'clock transport hasn't turned up - again! I dumped half the stuff from my Bergen at Club Brcko yesterday as we were told we may have to tab (walk) the last 10-15 kilometres in so I repacked it in case we go today. It was 1:30pm when the transport finally showed. I asked the driver if we were going today but he just shrugged his shoulders, so I put on my stubborn head and told him to come back for me when they decided to send us, and then went back to the bar. The other three left with the driver after trying to talk me into going, which turned out to be my mistake! I had a couple of beers then spent most of the day sunbathing and then went back to the bar in the evening, by 11:00pm the others had still not returned so I went to bed, again on the floor of the flat. At 1:20am I was rudely woken by the driver from Club Brcko, who told me that we were moving out tonight. Ten minutes later I was packed and we headed into Zagreb and the clubhouse. On arrival I was greeted by the trio and at last, issued with an AK-47 assault rifle, 4 grenades, a 64mm LAW (Light Anti-Tank Weapon, similar to the U.S. made 66mm), a steel helmet and 200 rounds of ammunition. We were also paid 5000 Dinars, about £12.50.

Our trip to Brcko was to be the long way round, which is believed to be the safest due to Brcko being behind Chetnik lines. We were to travel south from Zagreb to Split, and then

Myself and Radek, with the hearse in which we traveled through Bosnia. to

be an old Volkswagen Golf and, unbelievably, a black Mercedes hearse. With any luck none of us will return in it.

6.

We left Zagreb at 3:00am, our small group of three Brits and one Czech sat in the back of the hearse with two Croatians in the front and three Croatians in the Golf. The Croatians were also volunteers, some of them with family ties in the Brcko area. Two hours later at Karlovac our two vehicles were stopped by the Military Police who decided to check out the authorisation of all the weapons we were carrying. It was found that we had five grenades over our permitted allowance, so Broadmoor decided to give two of them to the MPs as a gift! Then they let us continue our journey.

We drove on through the night, past Rijeka and then boarded a ferry to the island of Pag where the hearse decided to break down. After I had bled the diesel system and got it running again we found a garage where it was supposedly fixed, again it broke down, and, after me bleeding the system twice more we found a garage north of Zadar where another mechanic found that the problem was a cracked washer and replaced it. We set off once more and in the afternoon finally arrived in Split. The hearse had now gained a 'lived in' look with weapons lying around and what grenades that were not dangling off Broadmoors belt were rolling around loose in the rear compartment - maybe the hearse was a good choice of vehicle ! We stayed the rest of the day in Split trying to sleep or sitting in the cafes close by just waiting for nightfall so we could set off once more.

We started the journey again at midnight, soon crossing the Croatian/Bosnian border and then leaving the main road for the mountain tracks and roads heading north-east towards Zenica. Now that we were in Bosnia, Tom and I sat in the back of the hearse with our weapons at the ready, waiting for Chetniks to jump out at us from behind any and every bush. During the night the silencer fell off the hearse and it now sounded like a tank, if there are any Chetniks ahead, we certainly won't be surprising them! At 7:00am we stopped at a small roadside cafe, and on checking my map I realised that after driving all night we were only 18 miles inside the Bosnian border, I can only assume that our Croatian navigators had got us lost. In the early afternoon we reached Zenica where the local police directed us to a motel on the outskirts of town, apparently Chetnik patrols had been spotted further on and it was considered unsafe for us to continue. Whilst talking to the police Broadmoor traded another grenade for an AK-47 bayonet.

In our commandeered rooms it was time to clean our clothes and weapons and then shower, even though there was no hot water, it was welcome. After a good nights sleep, I got dressed, the clothes I had washed were still wet because it had rained during the night, but at least they were dust free. At 10:00am we were given permission to continue our journey, but later in the day we were still in the same area, after being stopped several times on different routes out because of Chetnik road blocks further down the roads. We (the Brits) asked if it was possible to crash through the blockades but I don't think our Croatian friends fancied the idea. Finally an almost secure route out was shown to us on the map; the only problem was that we had to pass within easy range of a Chetnik .50 calibre machine gun emplacement. Our eager team suggested going forward to destroy it with our rocket launchers; unfortunately this wasn't allowed because our weapons were only to be used in the area where we had been employed to defend. It seems as though each area of Bosnia is funding its own defences against the Chetniks. The 'Smile of the Day' came when, as we were approaching the danger area, our lead vehicle, the red VW Golf with the three Croats inside, decided to take the rear position to our trusty hearse and then once we had passed through the area, retook the lead again. Eventually we reached Tuzla and passed through and on, until we were stopped again by Bosnian military police and put up in another motel in the small town of Srebrenik.

I had another good night's kip, got up at 7:00am, had a cold shower, dressed and then found a cafe and we had a brew before setting off once more for our final destination. We arrived at the village of Ulice, just outside Brcko. Already we could hear the sounds of mortar and artillery fire, confirming that we had arrived in the front line area. We were met by a Frenchman called Gaston who informed us that this was to be our new home. He showed us to our accommodation, a deserted house that had belonged to a Croatian family prior to the war, now commandeered by the Croatian HVO army to house soldiers. Later we met the other foreigners here, when they came back from a training session. There was another Frenchman - Nikolas, a German - Andreas, a Canadian - Ron and three Brits - Dave, Toms mate also from Welwyn Garden City, Joe and Lars. So together with our group of three Brits and one Czech, plus another Frenchman called Francois based nearby in Jagodnjak, that now makes 12 in all, maybe the start of a new International Brigade?

We sat and talked with these lads and introduced ourselves and a bottle of brandy appeared. Joe, from Braintree is the only ex-British army soldier here apart from me, he was in 3RRF. Dave, Broadmoor, Tom and Ron are all ex-French Foreign Legionnaires; the three Frenchmen are all ex-French army; Radek the Czech did his National Service in the Czechoslovakian army. Andreas the tall German, and Lars who was from Dorset, have no military experience apart from what they have done here. This is Gaston's third war; he has previously fought in Thailand and Burma, obviously a bloke to listen to. Most of the older hands here fought at Vinkovci in Croatia, and Nikolas was with the International Brigade in Osijek. Broadmoor has been steadily getting drunk and unfortunately has not given a good first impression of himself. He has just re-appeared with a skinhead hair-cut, shaven down to the wood, clutching a chicken which he has just murdered and has decided he is going to eat it tonight. It was this evening he collected the nickname Broadmoor, with questions on whether he may have escaped the institution.

I am now back at our new billet writing the diary that I have decided to record my trip by candlelight. I have turned down Broadmoors offer of some chicken, as have the others; although I am feeling hungry I can wait until tomorrow. I got up at 7:00am and made a brew on the fire I've just made outside. Tom is not feeling too good today; he keeps fleeing to the toilet. My guts aren't perfect either, it must have been the booze last night, I'm not a spirit drinker but I knocked back a fair bit. Another brandy casualty is 'Baldy Broadmoor' who hasn't surfaced yet. Later in the morning we received a briefing from our new commander Jelenic, a Croatian captain from Vinkovci, he informed us that all next week, starting from early tomorrow we would be carrying out reconnaissance and hit and run patrols. This afternoon we would be practising formations and signals, trying to fit in with the older hands. We were also told that our trip through Bosnia to here had been a first, and many had been amazed we had made it through - now they tell us!

Lars and Joe

In the evening we received a patrol briefing, we (the four new guys) were to be a rear protection party along with Lars and Joe, for the main recce team consisting of the older hands. We had worked out patrol positions earlier and hand signals, but it is mostly British Army orientated which is OK for me. I am carrying an RPG 7 rocket launcher as well as my AK-47; Radek is my number two and will carry three rockets. I had to familiarize myself with this weapon earlier and dry fired it. It was bed early that night ready for a 2am start; I could hear the town of Brcko only six miles away getting a good hammering from Chetnik artillery, mortars and heavy machine guns. Today the 9th July is my birthday - 35 years young today! We were up at 2:00am and got ready for the patrol, leaving Ulice at 2:30am, faces blackened and all our kit secure and silent. We picked up two local Croatian scouts and dropped off from our vehicle at Donji Vuksic and patrolled out to the main road near Brcko, north of Lanista.

On the way out we nearly shot two of our own scouts, as they had approached our RV position from the wrong direction, apparently we at the back of the patrol had not received the message to expect them, so when they turned up out of the darkness, walking down the track we were on, at first I thought they were the forward men of a Chetnik patrol. I was glad that when they were challenged the mix-up was sorted out, as to have shot two Croatians on our first patrol would not have been a good start. I was amazed at their casual attitude, as we were now supposed to be within 500 metres of the main Chetnik held road. On reaching the main road itself our rear protection group settled into defensive positions 50m away, while the main recce team crawled forward slowly checking for mines and booby traps until they reached the roadside itself. While they were at the roadside the two Chetnik guards strolled past with their weapons over their shoulders, too casually for my liking, they walked right past the recce team only two metres away not knowing how close they had come to their end, but they weren't killed as the idea of this patrol is to find this safe route from our lines and then possibly ambush a convoy at a later date. We were away from the area by first light and as we moved back towards our lines dawn was breaking, I was wary of a possible sniper attack or ambushes, as previously in this area they had been hit, with the loss of two Croatians. The roads and hedgerows on our route back had supposedly been mined by both sides, though I never saw any until one of our own roadblocks made up of a ploughing machine and an articulated truck and trailer left across a road 50 metres away from our own positions, under these vehicles four large anti tank mines had been positioned.

At one of the scout's houses we were treated to fried eggs, bread and Turkish style coffee by his family, I am now even happier they were not mistakenly shot earlier that night. We got back to Ulice at 10:30am and I cleaned and oiled my AK-47 and the RPG 7 and then got my head down. We had another briefing that evening, we are going out early again tomorrow. I have the RPG again, this time Broadmoor is my rocket carrier, as Radek is taking a sniper rifle. It was a two o'clock call again this morning. Went through the ritual of checking equipment and camming up (blackening faces and hands), onto the truck and away again by 2:30am. This time we were tasked to recce the area of Markovic Polje just to the right of the area we were in yesterday morning. Half of the village of Markovic Polje is supposedly held and patrolled by Chetniks, the other half patrolled by Croatians, although the village was deserted. Each side patrol their own halves from time to time and occasionally snipe at each others patrols, but the village is not thought to be permanently manned by either side as it is situated in the middle of no man's land. Our task this morning was to move into the Chetnik half of the village to find out and confirm there is no permanent Chetnik presence inside the village.

As we patrolled out again on foot towards the village we almost had another 'blue on blue' (two friendly patrols firing on each other), when a four man Croatian patrol came up behind us. Half of our patrol had crossed a bridge when Tom, the 'tail end charlie' of the patrol, called me back to say he had heard movement and talking 100metres to our rear. I passed the signal back up the patrol line to warn of possible enemy presence, and settled into the undergrowth and waited. The sound of approaching men was now easily distinguishable as the gravel crunched under their feet as they came closer, when they were less than ten metres away, they came out of the darkness in a group to find me stood in front of them, my AK 47 in my shoulder, when one of them saw me he shouted 'Stoi' (Stop) to his comrades and froze, with what happened last night in my mind, I said 'English' and they visibly seemed to relax, by now I could hear my own heart thumping. They seemed as pleased as we were that we had avoided another nasty situation as it was another close thing. Tom told me later that he could see himself firing into them if they had moved another inch after I'd challenged them, for him they were already dead. We should do something about the recognition of friendly troops approaching us from the rear, especially when one of them had a bushy beard and hair and another was wearing a Chetnik helmet (Chetniks are commonly thought of as bearded men). The patrol carried on crossing the demolished bridge which had only a foot wide spar remaining of the centre of the bridge across the river. When my turn to cross came, I stood on the spar not knowing how far it was to fall as it was still dark, I got halfway across it, still trying to keep my balance when the RPG 7 swung off my shoulder and swung round onto my chest causing me to lose my balance, I nearly fell into the river below but somehow managed to scurry across, two scares in as many minutes, my heart won't stand up to this sort of work. Finally, when Tom crossed, we moved off again and into the village, our rear protection group moved out to the left of the houses to a small copse overlooking the Chetnik half of the village, and we lay and watched the recce team move silently forward checking the houses for signs of any permanent positions.

Dawn was breaking as they cleared the houses, we covered the recce team for nearly an hour until they completed the task, during that hour we provided hundreds of mosquitoes with their breakfast - us! Once the task had been completed and no sign of a Chetnik presence had been found, we slowly moved out and filtered back towards our lines. This time at the bridge, I waited for Broadmoor to cross, before throwing the RPG to him, then crossing myself, although I don't know which is worse, crossing it in darkness or daylight when you can see the river flowing swiftly below. The rest of our return to our lines was uneventful and on our return we were treated to several cups of Turkish coffee and met the four Croatians who had bumped into us earlier in the night. It was translated to us that we had frightened the life out of them, I admitted to them, as did Tom that our heart rates also rapidly increased at the time!

We got a lift back to Ulice, our base, at 9:00am on a trailer pulled by a tractor, as Ron had driven over a spiked caltrop earlier on the way out and both rear wheels of our truck had been punctured. We have been told we may have to go on an ambush later this afternoon, so I had a wash, got some breakfast down my neck and went to bed.

I slept for a couple of hours and got up at midday, made a brew, cleaned my weapons and sorted out my kit for the ambush patrol, only to be told at four o'clock that it was off until maybe tomorrow, but I am already learning these are two of the most favourite words here, and have little meaning. That evening we sat around a campfire with a couple of bottles of brandy passing our previous personal histories. By 11:00pm I'd had enough and tottered off to bed, at least there was no early morning patrol tomorrow.

7.

I felt slightly hung over the next morning. We have been told we have no work on today and we are getting a days leave pass to go to Srebrenik, a town we passed through on our way here, which is rumoured to have beer. The pass and day off is mainly for the older hands but we are going as well. By 2:00pm with leave passes still in hand we still had no transport to get there, so it was called off. The older hands are now a bit disgruntled -

I don't blame them. They have now got a couple of bottles of brandy and gone back to their house.

By the early evening Dave and Ron decided they no longer want to work for this village and are planning to move tomorrow to another village called Donji Vuksic, just a couple of miles away. Whether it's the brandy talking or the cancelled day off was the last straw for them I don't know, but they think they would be better off working in Donji Vuksic. Personally I hope the move doesn't happen and tomorrow they will change their minds, but up to now Tom and Radek say they are going with them and I have been asked as well. Although I feel it would be better to stay together, I will go with them as I came here with Tom and Radek. Broadmoor has decided to stay in Ulice with Joe, Lars, Nikolas, Gaston and Andreas. The next morning the mood has still not changed and the move is still on, Dave and Gaston have been to see Jelenic who has OK'd the move, although it has been agreed to work together for large operations, but for now our new five man group is to come under the control of the local commander at Donji Vuksic.

At 4pm our kit was packed and loaded onto our truck, we also took the 82mm mortar and its 75 rounds, as apparently I am the only one who knows how to use it, although only in theory not in practice! Our new commander is a Croatian who originates from Donji Vuksic, called Boby, who met us on our arrival at the village and my first impression of him is a good one, he seems very friendly, helpful and pleased to have us here. He showed us to our new home, a large well furnished house, the five of us each have our own room. The house is good but obviously still has no electricity or running water. Tom, Radek and Ron have found a room each upstairs, Dave and I chose a room each downstairs. In the evening we were invited to a pig roast, as the cookhouse here in this village does not operate on Sunday evenings. We met the majority of the local garrison, or those who were not on guard, Drago, one of the Croatians we arrived here with (the hearse driver) is also based here, he's OK, and probably the only one of them I really got on with. I went back to our new home later and was in bed for 11:00pm.

I went to test the new cookhouse food next morning; it was the same menu - stew, but maybe slightly better than the cookhouse at Ulice. Then I spent the rest of the morning sewing extensions onto the pockets of my combat jacket, so that they could hold AK magazines, and sewed elastic grenade holders onto it, this would make it more comfortable for me to carry my ammunition than wearing the webbing we had been given. Later that afternoon we were all invited for a few drinks at Boby's house as it's his birthday today. I was not really in the mood for it and an hour later, Radek (who doesn't drink alcohol) and I returned to our house where I finished off my jacket alterations. I can now carry two magazines taped together on my rifle, one magazine in each top pocket, a magazine in my tail pocket, totalling five (150 rounds), two hand grenades held by the elastic holders. My jacket is now my webbing. In the evening the pair of us rejoined the others who were steadily getting drunk, especially Tom, who an hour later decided he wanted to argue with everyone. Radek and I decided to take him back to our new home; I admit he was a bit dodgy to be with, a good drink in him and walking up a dark road with a loaded AK 47, a round up the spout and him thinking Chetniks are behind every bush. Our first night here, or full day at least. I wonder what the locals are thinking of us already.

Up the next day at 8:00am, after breakfast today we are due to train with some of the locals. I'm not impressed with that idea. After the training session, which involved house clearing and basic patrolling, hand signals and other basic manoeuvres, I walked up the road to see the other lads at Ulice. They had been out early twice this morning in the Dubrava area and ambushed a small Chetnik convoy. On their return they were mortared but suffered no casualties, they managed to close the road, a main Chetnik supply route, for over an hour, and were going back again this afternoon. I didn't feel like telling them that we had just been training with the locals. In the afternoon, as we rummaged in the local scrap yard near Jagodnjak for two new tyres for our truck, the Ulice team went past us, as they went out on the operation.

Later in the evening we were hurriedly told, 'kit on, tool up, and be ready to move in five minutes.' We were quickly told as we threw our kit onto the truck that Francois' group from

Jagodnjak had heard a tank in their area, our group and his have been tasked to find and destroy it if possible. On arrival in Jagodnjak, we were given a fuller briefing which was basically that the tank has been in a static position for a day, according to local scouts, on the main Chetnik held road the other side of the village of Polijaci. We were to leave at 3:00am and recce the area, and if possible find and destroy the tank. We would stay here tonight in the house Francois lived in. Francois, being a Frenchman, had his own little supply of wine, which we helped him empty a couple of bottles of course. As we sat around talking and drinking his wine, one of the conversation pieces was about the German woman doctor in Ulice, she has apparently been feeling stressed lately and people were worried about her mental state. I myself had seen her while I was in Ulice for the couple of days, walking along the main street talking to herself. Today she went one better, we had heard that she was on the main street washing her backside and shouting at people who stopped to watch. She has now been moved to a hospital in Tuzla with a suspected nervous breakdown, now there is no doctor in this area.

We got up at 3:00am, dressed, cammed up and got our kit sorted for the mornings patrol. We teamed up with Francois' group who were carrying an OSSA Anti-Tank weapon (Similar to the NATO 84mm Carl Gustav anti tank weapon). We drove out to a drop off point near our own front line, and patrolled out on foot in single file out through no-mans land towards the Chetnik lines and the main road, moving cautiously as we neared the road, as along the roadside are manned bunkers every 200m, each bunker has one or two men inside guarding the road and the area in front of it. We moved into a small wood which ran along side of the road, and now had to creep, and virtually feel, our way through the wood, as broken twigs and branches lay underfoot which had to be moved as we slowly moved along. The job was made harder as the wood was believed to be mined. After an hour and a half in the wood, with no sign of the tank, we began to move back as it would soon be light and then in the daylight, and going back across the open ground, we would easily be spotted by the Chetnik bunkers. We returned slowly but safely back to our drop off point as dawn broke and were treated to our now customary coffee at a local scout's house. We hadn't discovered a tank in this area, but we now know that the wood we had been in was not mined and this would be valuable information for future operations. After the coffee we drove back to Jagodnjak and had breakfast there - stew. Our truck had been taken away for some repairs and to have the tyres replaced.

While waiting at Jagodnjak we were told some bad news which mainly affected the older hands. Milo, an Australian-Croatian who had been working with this group and had been captured a month earlier, had died as a prisoner. It seems that after a month of continual beatings and interrogations Milo eventually died. The group is sad and angry. Dave had been close to Milo and has taken it badly. At 4:00pm there's still no sign of our truck, Radek and I decided to set off on foot back to Donji Vuksic some 5 miles away. After 2 miles we managed to get a lift back to the village. After tea (more stew), I had a good strip wash and made a brew, then sat outside talking with Radek and Drago who had popped in to see us. Dave, Ron and Tom came back at 9:00pm and told us we may be going to Brcko tomorrow. We are going there to support the Bosnian Army. I don't know why really, as according to the latest reports the town has all but fallen, with the fighting now confined to the outskirts.

I got up at 7:30. This morning we are to prepare and check our equipment prior to our move to the besieged town of Brcko. We have been issued gas masks as the Chetniks are known to be using CS gas in the area. We are due to be picked up by Francois' group at midday, I am feeling a bit apprehensive about our move to the large town because all the stories are of heavy fighting, I know from my own army training that street fighting brings a heavy casualty rate. Our unit of five, plus Francois' group from Jagodnjak of eight men makes unlucky thirteen. Thirteen men is not a strong force to get involved in such battles, but apparently today's trip is just to see if there is anything to get involved in the near future - a reconnaissance mission of sorts, or so we are to believe. By 1:30pm Francois' group has still not turned up. Thinking the trip was off; our team started digging a mortar pit at the rear of our house for the 82mm mortar we had brought from Ulice. At 2:30 when we had a good sweat on from digging in the heat, sod's law decided that Francois and his group should turn up, whereupon they apologised for being late and enquired if we were ready. Putting our kit on again, we boarded their Mercedes pick up truck and headed towards Brcko. We travelled along dirt tracks and back roads for nearly an hour, the sounds of fighting in the town getting louder until we eventually arrived at the outskirts of the town. Once the truck had been safely parked behind a house we set off on foot to a forward control house only 200 metres inside the town perimeter. The sounds of rifle and machine gun fire could be clearly heard just ahead of the area we were moving into.

At the safe house we were told that the forward edge of the battle was 300m further on. I could hardly believe it, they (the Bosnians) were fighting for the last 500m of the town. Although we were officially here for a recce, we were carrying among other weapons the OSSA anti-tank weapon. The Bosnian (BIH Army) commander wanted to know if the group would go forward and use this on a heavily fortified sniper's bunker which was causing a lot of problems. Our recce has now been turned into a combat mission! We moved forward, dashing from house to house, staying low and moving very fast across gardens and crossing paths to avoid the sniper fire and ricocheting rounds which were now screeching around us. Finally we made it to a position at the side of a house on our forward line. Down the road, 150 metres away was the enemy sniper's position and Chetnik troops in the houses facing us. Machine guns and rifles were now firing in both directions and incoming rounds were hitting the house above us or cracking over our heads as we lay in whatever cover we could find. The sniper was located inside a house on the second floor and had a good view of our position. The Chetniks had fortified the position with sandbags and rubble so ordinary small arms fire had no chance of penetrating it. The sniper would be quite snug inside his bunker, firing through a small hole in the house wall. The plan was that on a given signal the group would fire bursts into and around the Chetnik positions, hoping to keep their heads down for a few seconds so that Brale, an English speaking Croatian in Francois' group, could get into position, sight and fire at the sniper's bunker with the OSSA. This rocket would almost certainly destroy, or at least seriously damage the bunker and hopefully kill the sniper. As we slowly crawled into firing positions ready to give fire support there was a lull in the shooting. Brale decided to fire before we were ready, and fired the rocket which exploded in the lower area at the front of the house, he had rushed the shot and missed by firing too quickly. The sniper must have decided not to hang around in his bunker though in case we fired a second rocket and he bugged out of the rear of the building. After another minute we decided to pull back in case the Chetniks decided to mortar our position. We were wrong. As we pulled back we could hear the rumble of a tank moving towards our line. The tank, probably a T55, ground its way into a position unseen by us but from where it could fire into the house we had just vacated. It fired directly at the house, then at the houses surrounding it. The noise was deafening as each round scored direct hits on the houses, the shrapnel from the shells and pieces of brick and concrete flew through the air and landed around us as we darted back to the HQ 300 metres behind us. The tank fired ten rounds, trying to hunt out our position before stopping and moving position again. After a couple of minutes it fired another 14 rounds of high explosive, again into the houses on our forward edge. Some of these houses which had already taken two or three hits began collapsing, bringing up large clouds of dust which hung in the air. Small arms and machine gun fire now hammered all around us. Back inside the HQ we waited for further instructions from the Bosnian commander but he decided against anymore offensive action for the time being. We were already learning that the Chetniks firepower was far superior to ours; we had fired one rocket and received twenty-four tank shells in return, we had also taken three casualties, all local BIH soldiers, who had been caught in one of the houses hit by the tank. All were shrapnel wounds; they were treated and then sent back to the medical aid centre further to the rear. As we waited in the nearly demolished HQ for further instructions Tom and Ron had found a pool table, so Radek and I challenged them to a game of doubles. We have now heard that we may be going back later to see if it is possible to hit the tank.

Brale is not looking too happy at the moment; he has just been given a bollocking by Francois for firing earlier, before he should have done. I feel sorry for him because I don't think I would have liked to have stood up with the OSSA on my shoulder in full view of the enemy and then took time with the shot, although I think that if he had waited for us to fire he may have had more time and been safer.

An hour later it was decided we should return to Donji Rahic before dark because the tank was now well back behind their lines and we wouldn't be able to get at it. We had upset the Chetniks though, and now they may think that the Bosnians have been supplied with anti-tank weapons and would be more cautious from now on.

(L to R) Radek, myself and Tom in a Tank damaged house in Brcko, North East Bosnia.

We returned to Donji Vuksic via the town of Donji Rahic where we stopped for a very welcome drink of cold orange and some molten ice-cream. Once back at our house it was time to clean our kit and then go to bed, exhausted.

8.

Got up late today at 9:30. Dave has gone to a remembrance mass being held this morning for Milo. We were told by Gaston that a Scotsman, an ex-legionnaire, had come to join the group. On finding out we were in Brcko he went straight out to join us. He got to Brcko with a team of Bosnians sent to reinforce and replace the casualties. As soon as he got there he tried to find our group, but as he moved up the line he was killed by a sniper with a single shot to the head. Why he couldn't wait until we had returned I don't know, apparently he had told the lads at Ulice that he had come for action and wanted to get stuck in straight away; at least he wouldn't know what hit him. We don't know what has happened to the body, nobody even knows his name, and they only know that he was a Scotsman who had been in the Legion for ten years.

At 11:00am we re-started digging the mortar pit until it became too hot to work. Tom, whilst digging, has been bitten or stung by something nasty. He looks half dead, his lips have gone numb, his eyes have puffed out and he's got a big lump on his leg where whatever it was got him. He will try anything to get out of work! When it got too hot to dig I started on building us a shower, just a simple but effective one, by tying three long poles together and standing them up tepee-style and hanging a bucket from them with small holes in the bottom. An easy job and everyone seems happy with it. In the evening when we had all played with the shower, we felt better and cleaner. Tom has recovered, especially now that we have purchased two bottles of brandy. Boby has come round with a new toy for me, a .308 SSG Austrian Steyr sniper rifle complete with a five round magazine and cross haired sniper scope. It is a very nice piece and feels well balanced. There are only twelve rounds for it at the moment but he has promised me more soon.

As the evening wore on Tom got drunk again and has gone off to bed clutching his AK-47. I don't think anyone trusts Tom at the moment with weapons when he's had a few. Boby, the local Croatian commander spent the evening with us and we all got to know him better. Dave has worked with Boby before, which is why he wanted to come to this village, when the group split a few days ago. Got up at 2:30am to take a leak. I didn't even get to the toilet door before I heard Tom get up with his rifle. He must have heard me moving across the landing, so he sat up in bed with his rifle and took off the safety catch - this guy is crazy! I hope that if I get shot and killed here, that someone takes the time to see if it was the Chetniks that got me or Tom! I went back to bed only to be awoken again by Ron at 6:15am, who had heard a light plane flying low above the house; it was quite possibly a Chetnik/Serbian JNA spotter plane. If it was, it almost certainly saw the mortar pit we had been digging at the rear of the house and it was decided it must be finished today. Although I don't think that a single 82mm mortar would worry them too much, but it is nice to watch Dave panicking after his alcohol injection last night, he wants this done, that done and everything else done! Now! It's nice not to have a hangover. I am seriously starting to wonder what I have let myself in for coming here, although I had to really laugh later, as Dave drove off in the truck to find out more information about the plane from the local HQ, when Ron asked where he had gone, red eyed Tom leaned over the balcony and said, 'probably gone to bury the truck!'

After a brew and our morning ritual of stoning the stray pigs, which visit us regularly to dig up the garden and generally wreck everything we have built or left out, we continued to dig the trench for the mortar pit which was finished, apart from the top cover, for 11:30am. Once the pit was finished I am going to concentrate on sorting out my kit and cleaning my two rifles, as we are told that tomorrow we may be going back to Brcko, this time for a couple of days. What we are going to do there I don't quite know, but as I wrote this entry into my diary I could hear the fighting from the town six miles away. In the evening we went up to the north position of the village for another pig roast with the locals. They managed to find us a cold bottle of Tuzla beer each which went down well; all the talk is of our forthcoming trip to Brcko tomorrow. The young local Croatian lads were trying to get a place with us but I think we can only take five of them, plus our team of five Tom, Dave, Ron, Radek and myself. Boby is cursing us because his lads are begging him to come tomorrow, they have heart but I don't think the next few days will be a picnic. I will not be surprised in the morning when we are due to leave to find a couple of eager stowaways. An early night tonight.

Up at 3:30am, I got dressed and made all of us a coffee before leaving for Brcko an hour later. Our five man team plus maybe six volunteers from the village, there should only be five of them but I keep counting six, and who am I to argue. I think Boby is going to be one man short for a day or two! I know some of the locals; Pepi-Joe, Mario, Matia and Drago (the hearse driver) plus Mico and his Second World War German MG 42 Spandau machine gun they have brought with them. We first drove to Ulice to meet up with Francois, Brale and another six of their group plus Gaston and Nikolas, from the Ulice team. Joe, Lars, Andreas and Broadmoor are staying behind. Joe and Andreas had been wounded earlier by a mine, Joe copping some in his side and Andreas in the knee, both are OK but Joe should really be in hospital.

We got to the outskirts of Brcko at around 8:00am. We are here to assist the BIH Army in dealing with some of the many Serbian snipers that are causing a high rate of casualties here. The first news is that we may now not be required as our very own Lord Carrington, from the U.K. has arranged an all party ceasefire (Serbia, Bosnia and Croatia) from 6:00pm this evening, only ten hours away. It is fairly quiet this morning, a change from our last visit, and we can hear only the odd round being fired from sniper positions, though not at us yet. I can't help thinking about the Legionnaire, the Scotsman, killed on his first day here not long ago. We took advantage of the calm to move up to the forward line of defence, from the HQ moving along the road in single file, wondering if and where the next shot was coming from. As we moved into our allocated positions, a line of near derelict houses, the Chetniks, realising the positions were being reinforced by us, started to shatter the calm. Heavy machine gun fire was directed towards us as we ran from house to house, dropping off groups at each house on the way. At one point we had to dash across a small road in full view of a Chetnik machine gunner, we moved rapidly across the open gap and dived behind the house one at a time, when it came to Dave's turn he ran across and the machine gunner

Moving up to Brcko with my AK4, and 64mm Anti-tank weapon on my back.

followed him bouncing rounds off the side of our house and above our heads as he had with each of us, only when he reached the relative safety at the rear of the house we were to move into he replied with a loud rasping fart! Suddenly we could not move for laughing. Once we had moved into the house we were to occupy, I set about building a firing position with Ron. Tom, Radek and Drago who were also reinforcing window and door positions so that incoming rounds would not cause us any damage once the position was secure. We could only work slowly now because the Chetniks were dropping mortars onto the line of our defence. The explosions, when close enough, shook the house and brought dust clouds drifting through it and also the occasional sniper or machine gun rounds could come through the windows and crash into the inner walls of the house, so we had to work mostly from the floor area, crawling around on our stomachs and staying below the windows, building up our fortifications. Upstairs in the front right hand bedroom I began chipping out a brick from the main outer wall until it came loose and I had a good view of the area to the front. The hole I had made in the wall was about two feet up from the bare floor, and I built a small area around the hole with furniture and mattresses for protection, I then found a car seat and a coffee table for a rifle rest and settled into my new sniper position. I carefully cleaned the scope of the SSG Steyr rifle, checked the magazine, and loaded a round into the breach and sat back watching. Ron would observe the area with binoculars and spot for me. The mortars stopped coming in after about 30 minutes and the heavy firing died down, with only a few exchanges of sniper fire. I fired about four rounds into doorways or windows where I had spotted movement, but so far they managed to keep their heads down, I hope my position is still unknown to them, as I only fired the single shots in five to ten minute intervals. Ron then spotted movement from the bottom right hand corner of a house around 300 metres away with a road behind it. I looked into the area through the sniper scope and saw a Chetnik soldier looking in our general direction. Only half his head was visible as he peered around the corner of the building, he didn't make a good target. I got him in my sights and waited, hoping he would show more of himself when suddenly another Chetnik soldier peered over the first one's shoulder, as he leant out to get a better view, he showed me his body and head from the waist up, I centered the cross hairs of the sight onto his chest and squeezed the trigger, the soldier flew backwards out of my sight and the first one disappeared as well. I don't know if I hit or killed him, but the shot and the chance was there, we focused on that area for another ten minutes but saw no further movement. After another half an hour in position I changed over with Ron and observed for a while, Ron fired two rounds into Chetnik positions to get the feel of the rifle and we continued to watch. Then minutes later I saw a Chetnik soldier dash across the road behind the house, where the two had been seen earlier, then another came, I directed Ron who watched through the sight, a third man ran across the road, Ron fired, the man stumbled forwards and went down out of sight. We saw no more movement from that area. Half an hour later the Chetniks started firing on fronts again with heavy machine gun, rifle fire, and mortars fire. Tom came upstairs to find out what we were up to; I was now back in my sniper position. Ron and Tom decided to test their AK's on automatic from the upstairs windows. I wish they hadn't bothered as the Chetniks now began to focus their attention on our house, and bullets were hammering off the brickwork. It was funny to watch as they returned fire burst for burst with the Chetniks; Tom had obviously been bored downstairs and was enjoying himself until we heard a tank rumbling towards our positions. It was time to go; the Chetniks had called up their armour which could fire safely but directly into our line of houses from behind their first line. I vacated my sniper position and followed the laughing Tom and Ron downstairs. They were quite amused at me gathering equipment together from my newly built position knowing that any minute it would or may be destroyed, the miserable sods! The tank began firing into the houses and as we left the rear of the house, the neighbouring house took a direct hit and blew apart as we ran through the gardens to a safer position. Tom and Ron became more amused at me running across back gardens and climbing fences as they watched me continually get tangled up in washing lines and trees by the barrel of my sniper rifle which was slung across my back.

We found a safer house, further back, out of the direct firing path of the tank. We settled in and caught our breath, Tom and Ron still highly amused at our last episode. Minutes later another team of locals, who came with us from Donji Vuksic, scrambled in, they had been very lucky. They had been inside their house when it took two direct hits from the tank. Pepi-Joe and Matia were covered in brick dust and had been hit on their heads by falling masonry. Neither of them had been hurt badly just lumps and bumps, Matia is one of those people who rarely takes chances and is always seen wearing his helmet, this time for once he had taken it off to eat his rations when seconds later he had debris bouncing off his head,. As we sat inside the house, CS gas began drifting through; the Chetniks had fired mortars and rifle grenades containing the gas. I grabbed my mask out of the pouch and put it on. The locals were having a few problems, they hadn't checked theirs before coming here and two of them still had them packed into the original plastic packing, by the time they had got them on their eyes were watering and they were coughing hard, but CS is only an irritant and they got over it fairly quickly, it was lucky for them that it wasn't a more deadly gas. Once the gas had cleared and the tank had gone we moved back into our old positions to check the damage. We had been hit upstairs but it wasn't too bad apart from a large hole in the upstairs front bedroom which had not been there earlier.

We had been seen moving back into our positions and the mortar rounds started to fall around the houses again. This time they were also using airburst shells which explode roughly 20-30 metres above the ground and spray the area below and around with red hot shrapnel. We stayed well into the shelter of our house. Towards the evening, after the shelling had stopped, we were engaged in a fire fight with some Chetniks in houses about 200 metres away from ours, I asked what time it was as I changed my magazines on my Kalashnikov AK47 rifle, the answer came 6:20pm - so much for the six o'clock ceasefire Lord Carrington! As it grew dark we all moved further back to safer and better defended positions, the shooting continued all evening and at 11:00pm I decided to get my head down for some sleep but was continually woken by Tom blasting off rounds into the darkness, at an unseen enemy.

9.

Woken up at 7:00am by Dave, who's not too happy this morning as Tom had been firing wildly in the darkness last night and some of his bursts of fire were hitting houses occupied by the local Bosnian troops, luckily no one had been hurt. Dave is going back to Donji Vuksic this morning with all the lads from the village, except Drago who is staying with Tom, Ron, Radek and me. After a quick breakfast of stew we moved back to the forward line and into the house occupied yesterday by Pepi-Joe and his gang, or what was left of it after it had been hit twice by the tank!

We had been sent to this position because it had a good view of a Chetnik sniper bunker which had been causing problems yesterday. Once in the building, we built and strengthened a sniper position of our own. Ron and I began to exchange shots with the Chetnik sniper, but it was obvious that we were not going to hit him as he was well protected and firing through a slit in the wall of a building some 350 metres away, the houses around him also had Chetnik troops in who were spraying our position with automatic fire every so often. We decided to try and hit the sniper's bunker with a 64mm LAW rocket launcher, so Radek and Drago went to see if they could find a good position to give covering fire from, while Tom, Ron and I kept the Chetniks busy with rifle fire. Half an hour later Radek and Drago had still not returned and I started to get a bit worried, to make things worse Tom had decided to start playing cowboy again, firing on automatic from the front of our house, seemingly oblivious to the fact that two of our men were out in front somewhere, so it was a great relief when five minutes later I saw Radek and Drago making their way slowly but safely back to the house, although they had failed to find a safe position for the rocket launcher. We decided to make the attack from behind an outhouse at the rear of our position; we could fire over it if we stood on top of an upturned wheelbarrow, though we may have been beyond the launchers maximum range. Tom volunteered to fire the rocket while Ron and Radek would give covering fire from our house while myself and Drago would do the same from the house next door. First we would have to crawl across 15m of open ground in full view of the snipers bunker. The plan was simple, once Drago and I were in position we would all fire automatic bursts at the Chetnik positions, hopefully keeping their heads down long enough for Tom to come up from behind the shed and fire the LAW which would be no easy task. Ron and Radek took up their positions in our building and covered Drago and I as we crawled next door, we arrived safely and found two firing positions with a good view of the Chetnik positions, then settled down to wait until 12:45 when I would initiate the attack. Minutes felt like hours until the time came and Drago and I began firing into the Chetnik houses. We fired bursts into windows and doorways of the houses they were in, and then heard the whoosh of our rocket being fired. After Tom had fired Drago and I got back to our house as quickly as possible where we joined the other three already waiting in the bunker. We believe the front of the house was only hit by shrapnel as the rocket fell short, and it didn't silence the sniper who let out a cheeky burst of fire in our direction and the Chetniks fired mortar after mortar on our line again though we were safe inside our bunker. Tom felt bad about missing but it wasn't his fault as it was the rockets maximum range, it was the first time he had fired this weapon and he was in an exposed position with not much time to fire. We moved back to the command HQ house at 2:00pm after the mortar and machine gun fire had died down. We had some food (stew) then decided between us to have another crack at the sniper; he was beginning to annoy us now.

When we returned to our position I decided to mount the attack at 4:00pm and I would fire the LAW. Ron and Tom would cover me from our building and Drago and Radek from the house next door. The plan would be exactly the same only this time Ron would initiate the attack. As 4:00pm approached I stood on the wheelbarrow behind the shed with the rocket launcher prepared and ready to fire. I could hear my heart thumping in my chest. When I heard the others firing I stood up and sighted the launcher onto the sniper position for what seemed like an eternity. I pressed the trigger on top of the launcher and it sped on its way and I jumped down behind the shed to safety, or so I thought. After a couple of seconds the rocket struck and exploded. This time though the Chetniks were more prepared, I went to the corner of the shed to cover Radek and Drago back across the open ground but mortars and rifle grenades were already exploding around us, and saw two rifle grenades explode on the front of their house. I saw them dive down the stairs and they sensibly stayed put under them.

Then a rifle grenade exploded about 10 metres behind me throwing shrapnel and debris everywhere, the blast pushed me into the wall and I felt the backs of my legs stinging and a chunk of rock hit me on the ankle. I rapidly retreated back to the bunker. Gaston, who had appeared a few minutes before the action, also fired a striker grenade (M79) towards the snipers position before joining me and the others inside our bunker. Radek and Drago were still stuck in the house opposite as mortars, rifle grenades and machine gun fire poured into our positions. However, the sniper did not cockily tap out his return fire - maybe we had sorted him this time. I pulled down my trousers and checked the backs of my legs for injuries, thankfully I had none, just lots of red welts where my legs had been peppered by gravel thrown up from the blast, I was also a bit deaf in one ear but hoped this would wear off - I had been very lucky and knew I had used up one of my lives today. After only twenty minutes of heavy incoming fire it mysteriously dwindled and then stopped, they may have had casualties to move, but at least it gave us forty minutes of peace in which to collect Radek and Drago and return to HQ. The houses to the left and right of the snipers bunker were on fire but we couldn't see through the smoke to check how much damage we had done to his position. The fires from the houses were either from the rocket, maybe tracer rounds or even started by the enemy to provide smoke cover.

As we pulled back the tank began firing into our houses from his hiding place, scoring direct hits every time, even worse was to come when at 8:00pm heavy artillery started raining down on us. This was heavy stuff, leaving fifteen feet wide craters in the ground and shaking the foundations of the houses we sheltered in, the noise was deafening, the earth shaking with each explosion. One scored a direct hit on the house we had fired the rockets from earlier completely destroying it. All we could do was return with rifle fire.

Got up around 7:00am after another night of shelling and small arms fire, but after yesterday I slept pretty well. At 8:00am we joined Francois' group for the return journey to Donji Vuksic. Before we left Francois told the Bosnian commander that we would be back in 7-10 days, and told us that we had hit and damaged the snipers house, the rocket had struck and penetrated the wall above the snipers position. The journey back took two and a half hours, with far too many stops for coffee and the Croatian commander's war stories for my liking, we all just wanted to get back and clean our weapons, our clothes and ourselves. We eventually got into Donji Vuksic at 10:30am and were told that we had the rest of the day off and were given passes to Srebrenik. Once cleaned and wearing fresh uniforms we got onto a truck and set off on the two hour journey over an overgrown mountain track to Srebrenik. By the time we arrived our fresh, clean uniforms were covered in dust, twigs, leaves and insects though the first cold beer soon put a smile on our faces. The beer was going down well, and the meal we got - schnitzel and CHIPS! - was a bonus, but as the beer flowed the inevitable happened and there were drunks among us. As we drove out of Srebrenik, Matia, a local, decided to fire an automatic burst from his AK-47. This promptly brought our trucks to a halt and a very angry Francois and Gaston came back to find out who the culprit was, Matia was given a good bollocking in a mixture of French and broken English, most of which he didn't understand but he got the idea. I am on the side of the two Frenchmen so I didn't smile at him sympathetically as some of the others did when we moved on. The problem is that we are Croatian HVO troops in our Bosnian BIH allies area. They will have patrols and sentries in the area that would see two truckloads of strange troops and would have no idea who we are, especially as it is going dark and the uniforms look the same on all sides, an obvious avoidable threat. We were forced to stop again later when Angelo, another local, leapt off the back of our vehicle as we passed through a deserted Serbian village with the intention of setting fire to a Serbian church. Four or five of the others went to drag him back as I could see tomorrows local news headline, 'drunken Croat soldiers burn church', luckily it didn't happen. As we prepared to set off once more, a drunken Tom decided to fire a burst into the air from his AK-47 to impress the locals, this was totally unprofessional, dangerous and stupid, and Gaston and I told him so, we were supposed to be setting an example to these people as 'professional' soldiers. We set off back to Donji Vuksic on a calmer and quieter truck. I knew that I may end up falling out with Tom when we got back but I wasn't worried, I was inwardly very angry with him and his cowboy attitude when he'd had too much drink. I don't think he realises the danger he puts us in when he acts like this, he almost got himself and Radek killed two days ago on a failed tank hunt in Brcko plus the other incidents when he was guilty of firing indiscriminately onto Bosnian positions on more than one occasion. I am not exactly impressed at this moment with the ex

- Legionnaire. Finally arriving back in Donji Vuksic we dropped the locals off and went back to our house. I took off my kit, put my AK away and went outside to make a brew and boil some eggs. Tom, now in disgrace, went off to his room and to bed. Before I went to bed at midnight I heard firing from the south of our village and wondered what the drunken locals were doing now. Not a good day off.

Got up at 8:30am without a hangover so I know I wasn't drunk yesterday. Dave was outside making a brew and I asked him what the plan was for today. He is training some of Boby's lads (the locals) later, anybody who wanted to help could, and those who didn't had a free day. I told him not to count me in as I wanted to go up and see the Ulice team about working with them. Dave asked me not to think about leaving the Vuksic team but said that it was OK to work with the Ulice team for a while as he would be involved with training the locals for the next few days. He also said that I could use the truck if I needed it. As I left Donji Vuksic, on my way to Ulice, I was stopped by Boby, the Donji Vuksic commander, who was not looking a happy man. He told me that the shooting I had heard last night was some of his lads who had returned with us. They had gone in to six deserted Serbian houses nearby and set fire to them and shot several stray pigs and he is now trying to get a lift into Ulice with me to do some explaining to 108 Brigade 2 Battalion HQ; he also ended up fighting with Angelo, his brother, giving him a black eye. I didn't say anything about Angelo wanting to set light to the Serbian church en route back last night, in any case I don't think we will get another trip out to Srebrenik in the near future.

On the way into Ulice Boby told me that reports had filtered back that our Brcko trip had been a success. The Serbs had pulled their front line back by two hundred metres, mainly because they were in reach of our 64mm LAW rockets we had used that day on the sniper position and during the days fighting, they had twelve casualties, either dead or wounded. These figures are known by the monitoring of the Serbian radio messages, I don't really know how I feel at the moment about my part in the actions but I know it is rather them than me. Boby also suggested that we use the pigs killed last night for a barbeque and asked me to invite the Ulice team down. We met

Gaston, Joe, Lars and Broadmoor at Ulice, Nikolas and Andreas are asleep. Gaston has planned an operation in Dubrava for tomorrow so I've asked to join him. I've passed on Boby's invitation and I will get more information on the operation at the barbeque tonight. They have all heard about Tom's escapades last night from Gaston and various comments have been made so at least I don't need to moan about it.

The roast pig on a spit, that evening, went down well with the four crates of beer funded by our Mr. Broadmoor who had acquired them through his wheeling and dealing activities. He had arrived with the other five from Ulice. Francois and Brale had turned up from Jagodnjak and Boby was here with Pepi-Joe and Matia. I've supplied a bottle of Brandy I bought in Ulice but I'll stick to Broadmoor's beer tonight as I have an early start in the morning. Gaston has given us a rough outline of orders; we will be preparing and fortifying positions between Dubrava and the Chetnik held main road for the next two days in preparation for an attack on a convoy of supply vehicles for the town of Cerik, which is believed to have tank support.

We were away from Donji Vuksic in our truck by 7:30am, and picked up Gaston's team from Ulice and set off to Dubrava via Jagodnjak. We arrived at the church in Dubrava around 9:00am and it was already getting hot as we unloaded our kit from the truck. The main base HQ in Dubrava, was the buildings in and around the church grounds, this wasn't a good choice as the church steeple, which had already taken a few hits, was an excellent target indicator for the Chetnik machine gunners and mortar men, who were only 1200m away on the main road which they held to the west of us. We moved cautiously up to our forward positions manned by local Croatian soldiers. These were three deserted houses on the outskirts of Dubrava some seven hundred metres from the church with only open sparse ground between them.

Once we got to these houses, we could see the main Chetnik held road which ran between Cerik and the Chetnik stronghold of Pelagicevo. The houses were on a forward slope on higher ground than the road which was a hundred feet below, but still five hundred metres away with some dead ground between our position and the road. We began the task of digging protective bunkers and positions to fire from, behind and to the sides of the houses. It was now getting very hot and the sweat began pouring out of us as we dug, last nights beer was on the move, most of it dripping into my eyes. By 2:00pm we were all exhausted and it became too hot to carry on. Gaston decided we should pack up and make another early start tomorrow morning. I put my shirt and my helmet back on, slung the sniper rifle across my back and picked up my AK-47 just as the Chetniks decided to hit our positions with rifle and machine gun fire. We had to run and crawl the 700 metres back across the open ground to the relative safety of the church HQ, already tired and drained from the mornings digging, this didn't help at all, but with rounds cracking overhead we managed to find the strength in us.

Once all back safely at the church, Pelec, our local scout for the day, took us down to the canteen and there waiting for us was a meal of bread, cottage cheese, fried eggs, pork belly and of course coffee. For a meal like this everything we had done today was worth it.

We returned back to Donji Vuksic after dropping off the Ulice team, except Gaston who came back with me to see Dave about getting some more of the Vuksic team to come out and help tomorrow. Once back I was greeted by a brown greyhound dog which had apparently turned up this morning. It has an injured leg, and Radek has treated, fed and watered it and it seems to have decided to stay. Dave has told Gaston he can take the other three of our team with him tomorrow, that is Radek, Tom and Ron but unfortunately I have to stay behind with Dave in case of any unlikely call out, as I had been out playing today. Later in the evening we sat around a fire in the garden talking. I told the lads what to expect at Dubrava in the morning, and also told them that I will have built a warm shower by the time they return from finishing off the positions tomorrow afternoon. I will also have to dispose of a dead pig that we have just found by following our noses, laying at the bottom of the garden, I thought it was Dave giving off the stink!

"Dog" and Me

It has started to bloat so it will have to go. Hopefully our new pet will keep them away in the future; we have decided to call him DOG

10.

Got up at 6:00am, went outside to light a fire for the morning brew, Dog seemed glad to see me, he's obviously happy to stay and the garden is pig free apart from the dead, smelly one!   I went to Ulice in the truck to collect Gaston's team and bring them here for coffee before they set off for Dubrava. Dave and Broadmoor are staying here to train the locals again today.

After they had all left I set about building us a shower after first towing the pig carcass with the truck as far away as I could before pouring diesel over the rotting pig and setting light to it. The shower was simple to build or at least modify. I dragged an old cooker up next to the shower unit as a base, built it up with bricks then placed a 50 gallon plastic drum on top for the water, connected a few pipes from the base of the drum to a shower handle and flex (stolen from the bathroom) and then proceeded to run up and down a ladder for half an hour carrying buckets of water from the well to fill the drum which now stands eight feet high. Hopefully the water will warm in the sunlight.

The lads arrived back in the mid-afternoon from Dubrava. While they carried out the work of digging and fortifying the positions they came under sniper fire, but nothing serious. I'm glad I didn't go as I've had a sore throat all day, it's probably these Yugoslavian cigarettes, and we get a free pack of 20 issued each day. Everybody has had a go in the shower; the water is warmer now so it works! Tom's return flight ticket expired yesterday so it looks like he's staying on whether he likes it or not, he seems quieter now that Dave has had a word with him, better that way as they are friends. After we had all showered, Tom and I went to raid the unoccupied house next door for coffee, sugar or tinned food but someone had beaten us to it. The house and its contents were more or less as its owners had left it, obviously not ransacked like some houses we had seen that had been visited by the Serbians/Chetniks.

Broadmoor came round later with some news; I was now officially a sergeant in the Croatian HVO Army. Not that rank means much here but it should upset my friend old Chris Tetlock when and if I get home as Chris was a sergeant during the Second World War.

Broadmoor was also sporting his latest acquisition, a flak jacket he's conned somebody out of. I have to admire him in a way, he's a brilliant scrounger.

The four of us left early the next morning from Donji Vuksic, Me, Tom, Ron and Radek set off in the truck to pick up the Ulice team of Gaston, Joe, Lars, Nikolas and Andreas. Dave and Broadmoor are staying behind again because they are still involved in training the locals. As we pulled into Dubrava HQ it was almost as if the Chetniks were expecting us. As we were jumping off the truck, 30mm or 50mm shells started exploding on the buildings or in the air above us. We all dived to the ground as I was introduced to the 'Praga' as it is called here, the 'Praga' is an armoured vehicle which is equipped with 30mm or 50mm cannons, primarily used as an anti-aircraft weapon, but as our side have no aircraft they have had to find another use for it. The barrels can be lowered and used against ground troops, and shells explode on impact and spray tiny fragments of shrapnel around the area, a very effective weapon, and very scary if your on the receiving end. After firing about a hundred rounds, several hitting the already battered church tower, the

Chetniks ceased firing. As I picked myself up from behind the tree I had hidden behind I sincerely hoped that they had stopped firing because they were low on this type of ammunition. It was my first time under this type of fire and hopefully my last, it's hard to explain but it was definitely scary. Each round cracks through the air as it passes you, which you would expect, but then the round explodes with a bang followed by zipping sounds as the shrapnel scatters around the impact area. Laying in cover and listening to the crack, bang, zip, zip, zip, and when about a hundred of these rounds are fired you get the feeling that nothing in the area could remain unscathed. The noise, as best I can explain it, is like listening to a stereo through headphones on full volume. Thankfully the focus of this fire was the church tower 50m to our right, as the firing lulled we ran towards the HQ buildings and waited until we were absolutely sure it was all over, then came the 700m dash and crawl race down to the prepared positions overlooking the road. The now alert Chetnik machine gunners were firing at anything that moved, but thankfully their firing from the road below us was usually high. We dived to the ground with each burst, and as every soldier will tell you, with every dive you usually land painfully on a stone sticking up out of the ground and then you have to push your helmet back up after it slides over your eyes, then you pick yourself up and start running again with all your kit - great fun!

The Church Tower at Dubrava

Once into our new positions we were only subjected to the odd round of sniper fire, none of which came close to hitting a human target. Our plan was to fire on passing Chetnik vehicles, hopefully annoying them enough for them to bring their armour out, maybe the Praga or a nice fat tank. Gaston could then get them in the sights of the BST anti-tank recoilless cannon and hopefully hit them.

Over the next few hours only four vehicles went past, three trucks and a jeep, all doing between 50-60mph. With only a 100 metre stretch of road to fire at them and at a distance of 500 metres our job was not at all easy. I did hit one truck with the sniper rifle but the AK-47 was ineffective, an AK on automatic is not entirely accurate, so although we may have hit more I can only be definite about one shot. At 2:00pm we decided to withdraw back to HQ as we obviously weren't annoying them enough for them to send out a tank to keep us quiet.

Our move back to the HQ buildings was unimpeded, and once back it was straight into the canteen to get out of the sun. After a good meal of fried eggs, tinned meat and fresh bread we decided to go down to the river at Bijela for a swim. The water was very shallow, but cool and refreshing. The only problem was that it had muddy banks and once we'd had a good splash about the inevitable happened - a mud fight. Five minutes later we were all covered with thick, slimy mud splats where we'd taken direct hits. Once a truce was in effect we all started to wash ourselves down, except for Andreas that is, who covered himself from head to foot in thick mud. When he had done this he made himself a grass loincloth, picked up a stick and started to dance around, demanding that we all do the same and then we could attack the Chetniks as a new band of natural warriors. This was all to the amusement of some local civilians who had been watching the lunatic foreigners 'swimming'. When he had calmed down he cleaned up and joined the rest of us for the trip back to Dubrava. We had decided to spend the night there so that we could have another 'go' in the morning. At the Dubrava HQ they had an unusual luxury, a portable black and white TV working off a truck battery. I think the Olympics were on, but I only managed an hour of this before I went to bed which was a room with six mattresses pushed together on the floor for the nine of us.

Got up at 5:00am. Somehow Broadmoor had arrived during the night complete with his newly acquired 7.62 Tokarev pistol.

Whilst showing it off he told us a rumour was going round the villages that Joe had been killed yesterday. I gave Joe a poke with my finger, and apart from needing his usual caffeine injection he looked okay to us. Well, alive anyway. By 6:00am we were back in our forward bunkers. This time I moved to another bunker sited between two buildings on the forward slope overlooking the road. I was sharing with Broadmoor which nearly turned out to be a bad decision. Before starting the morning's 'shoot' we first had to destroy a tree with plastic explosive to give the anti-tank weapons a clearer view of the road. As the morning wore on the Chetniks must have decided they had had enough of us shooting at their vehicles because they started using the 50mm shells from the Praga on us, although not from the road as we had hoped, but firing from behind a tree line out of our view, but where they could see our rooftops. This didn't affect us too much as we stayed well down in our bunkers. After we had annoyed them with some more rifle fire they started to mortar our positions from nearby Pelagicevo. As the 'plop' of the mortar being fired from the tube could be heard and it took about forty seconds for the bomb to reach us we had plenty of time to get into cover before they started exploding around us, we simply had to count the number of plops and you knew how many explosions there were going to be before you could come out of cover. I must admit that I enjoyed being mortared that morning, the excitement came from the threat of a direct hit, if you got one of those you wouldn't know much about it anyway, so why worry? During one of the mortaring sessions we could hear the Chetniks moving a tank up into position to fire.

After hearing three mortar 'plops', Broadmoor and I got into the bunker, to await the arrival of three incoming mortar bombs. I decided to light a cigarette while waiting for the rounds to land. At the same time the tank fired, I looked up at Broadmoor and then BANG! I was covered in dust as I threw myself on the floor of the bunker, dust was swirling around and I could smell burning plastic. I shouted to Broadmoor to see if he was alright. He replied with 'What the fuck was that?' I told him it was 'the fucking tank.' We weren't aware of the mortar bombs until they exploded because we had been deafened by the blast from the tank. I didn't feel safe, and I didn't feel excited anymore - crump, the third round went off. The dust was beginning to clear but the smell of cordite and burning plastic hung in the air. As I sat up I must have looked a sight, covered in dust with my unlit cigarette hanging from my mouth in tatters. Broadmoor sat up and looked at me with saucer eyes and shouted, 'Your fag's been blown in half.' In fact I'd broken it when I dived on the floor but I started laughing which started him off. As we were laughing more mortar rounds started to impact so he said, 'This is fucking stupid this, and somebody's going to get hurt'. 'Lets go and get a cup of coffee.' It took about five minutes to stop laughing - possibly shock and fear induced.

Although nobody was hurt that day it was my second really close call and hopefully my last. At 10:30am we headed back to the Dubrava HQ. Before we went, Broadmoor and I checked the front of our bunker. The tank round had impacted on the ground just in front of us and had blown away half the front layer of sandbags. The second and third layers had been splattered with hot metallic shards. The sandbags were plastic, soil filled fertiliser sacks, hence the plastic smell. One large piece of shrapnel had gone through one of the top bags and through the roof of the bunker. The only good thing about it was that it had gone through Broadmoor's side and not mine. We left the position once more disappointed at not having destroyed any of their heavy stuff. I did put a hole in another one of their trucks though. After another good meal of goulash, eggs and salad we set off back to Donji Vuksic.

Back at our house I was glad to get showered. Dog was there to greet us, and in the back garden a pig was being prepared for a barbeque tonight to celebrate a Bosnian holiday. Any excuse. The meal was very good, with vegetables prepared by Tom and Ron. The roast pig went down well with the three crates of beer supplied by Boby. At around 10:00pm the sing-songs started, the Brits stood up and sung the national anthem, closely followed by Legionnaire marching songs. The shock was to come from some of the local HOS militia men, who after about half an hour decided to join in. When they sang, it was with arms outstretched singing Nazi songs, and I began to wonder whether I was on the right side. The songs were in no way meant to anger us but they were sung with feeling and I didn't like it, and made comments during them to show my disapproval. I know the Serbians are meant to be the bad guys but I have to wonder what I am doing here after seeing this, especially when I almost got killed today fighting for these people. In the end though, their songs were drowned out by the

Foreign Legion marching songs that all the ex-Legionnaires know, I was glad about this even though I don't particularly like the French either. I sat outside with Radek and Dog at the end for half an hour before going to bed at 1:00am. Got up at 8:30am and went round the back to look at last night's mess, at least Dog had kept the pigs away, but we all got stuck in and it was cleaned up by 10:00am. We sat around relaxing until Boby turned up in a hurry and asked Dave to take us out to sweep the ex-Chetnik village his men had set fire to the other night. Boby told us that two Chetniks had been seen there and it was possible that they may be trying to either retrieve or store weapons there. We left on foot so that the local villagers would not know anything until we had gone, the fewer people who knew, the more chance we had of finding them. We quickly kitted up and moved out of our village and across the fields. We moved across country to a small village to the South of the target village. We found our scout outside his house with his family and friends preparing coffee in readiness for our arrival. Obviously he had not been told that this was a covert operation, he was more interested in making us welcome and finding places for us around his garden table.

Working with us today was going to put him on a higher social plane in the village so he was going to make the most of this, his day. Needless to say, the operation was probably blown and

Me returning from patrol with Steyr .308 sniper rifle, my AK47 on my back. Gaston is behind with the Striker grenade launcher.

the chance of capturing the Chetniks zero. An hour passed before we set off for the village a mile away. We moved into the outskirts of the village and started a systematic search of the houses. A small room underneath one of the houses was found to have been inhabited recently by one or maybe two people, but unfortunately our birds had flown. All the houses we searched had been previously looted, with clothes and furniture strewn about. Either that or they had been burnt out completely. Our only result came from a garden where Tom found a wire leading to a well. Attached to the wire was an old M48 rifle and five rounds of ammunition, all in good condition, well greased and oiled and wrapped in, of all things, a Marks and Spencer's plastic bag. After another two hours of fruitless searching the operation was ended.

Broadmoor lived up to his reputation and turned up with a one eyed horse he had captured. He set off on its back to Ulice with it, as possible trading material. I was glad to get back to a good shower and the chance to cool off., the heat of the day had taken it out of me, possibly something to do with last night's boozing. We had only been back an hour when Boby turned up with a new face who had just arrived from Paris. He was called John, a Brit from Stoke-on-Trent and an ex-Legionnaire friend of Dave's. He is now settling in with us as a new team member.

11.

I went for an hours nap at 7:00pm and woke up 12 hours later at 7:00am. Today is a day off, so this morning was my clean up morning. I cleaned and oiled my AK-47 and my sniper rifle, put two coats of dubbing on my newly acquired boots, dug my room out and washed my clothes. Radek, the crazy Czech has just bathed Dog who's riddled with fleas, he also sprayed him with fly-spray and when he tried to catch him to dry him, Dog went berserk, running around at a hundred miles an hour, in and out of everyone's room and eventually dived on to my bed, with my clean sheets and new (recently acquired) quilts on it. Why me? In the evening we were told to be up at 4:00am for a recce patrol in the Lanista and Markovic Polje areas, so I sorted my kit and got an early night.

Up at 4am and left for the morning's recce. In the Lanista area all seemed quiet and the local scouts verified this, further on as we moved towards Markovic Polje, we were stopped by local scouts from that area and told that during the night a large truck arrived which they thought had unloaded a tank. This they believed had happened on the main road just east of Loncari. Daylight was now creeping up, so it would not be safe to go any further towards the road for a 'look see'. It would mean moving over a mile of open land and we would certainly be seen. It was decided we will return tonight and set up two static listening patrols to confirm if it was a tank they have brought into the area and secondly to possibly pinpoint it's position. We arrived back at Donji Vuksic at 9am. Had breakfast (stew) and after getting washed and shaved went back to bed until 2pm. After some more stew at 6pm, I got ready for tonight's patrol. Broadmoor had arrived with Joe and Lars who will be working with us tonight.

The plan is that I will take out one patrol to the Drenova area and set up a listening post there. I will go with Boby in his pick up truck, and be dropped off with Tom, Radek, Ron, and John who will also be coming. Broadmoor will take Joe and Lars, to a position roughly between Lanista and Markovic Polje, in our truck and drop them off where they should link up with the local scouts and set up another listening post. Once this is done we will settle in and wait for the tank to move, if there is a tank and it does move or run its engines, both positions will take a bearing from our compasses on its rough position and hopefully if both teams take a bearing at the same time, we will be able to pinpoint it's position. We left Donji Vuksic at 8:30pm and drove across country until we were roughly 500 metres south of Drenova and moved into the village on foot. The village is deserted but as we moved into it a dog kept barking at us and being only 400 metres away from the main road and Chetnik first line, it was going to give us away. We were well within range of their machine guns and we were also on our guard in case they had any patrols out., so I crept towards the dog, I got to within a couple of feet from its face and gave it a belt of CS gas from a canister that I always carried in the arm pouch of my jacket (intended for use on taking prisoners and snatch patrols), it worked and the dog made a rapid retreat.

Once in position at the back of the village, we got down in all round defence and waited. The Chetniks were already getting nervous in their positions along the road and frequent gun bursts rang through the air as they shot at shadows but none close enough to our group to worry us. In fact it was quite comforting to think as we watched lines of tracer crossing the night sky that it was unlikely they had any patrols out forward of their line and if they had, hopefully it was them they were firing at. Luck was with us when, at 10:20pm the tank we were trying to find, started up, the engine noise clearly audible. The tank ran its engine for ten minutes, possibly charging its radio batteries; we took our bearing and began the uneventful move back. We arrived back at Donji Vuksic at midnight. Tomorrow we can work out its exact position from both bearings and hopefully get permission to take it out. In the morning I went for breakfast, stew for a change. I saw Joe and his bearing confirmed the tank position and all the information has been passed onto the HQ at Ulice but apparently we have been stood down today, why we haven't been tasked to go and hit it, I don't know. Joe and Lars suffered badly from a mosquito attack last night and both have the lumps to prove it.

I spent the day cleaning out my room again and sunbathing. What a lovely war! In the early evening I drove John into Ulice so he could buy a bottle of brandy for the lads. When we returned we settled down for a quiet drink and Boby with some of his lads, the locals, turned up with another bottle and a cow's liver which was promptly fried and scoffed. As we sat talking, Broadmoor turned up with Jelenic the Ulice commander who hurriedly had a discussion in Croatian with Boby. Broadmoor was proudly discussing his new acquisition, an ancient but working Zastava light truck. How does he do it? I am slowly getting used to the ways of the Bosnian and HVO Armies. Most of the time we are left standing around for hours not knowing what's going on, or we are told 'Kit on, tool up and move out in five minutes', still not knowing what's going on, and the latter is what we were told.

I quickly got dressed and grabbed my AK-47, the sniper rifle and my helmet and jumped on to the back of Broadmoor's new truck with the rest of the team. While Boby rounded up a few of the locals and followed in his pick up, towards the village of Bubanja just North of Bijela. Whilst on the move Dave quickly briefed us that the Chetniks had been putting heavy fire from small arms and mortars down on the area, the locals were getting edgy and feared an imminent attack. Our job would be to reinforce the guard there along with the Ulice team who had already been deployed, along with Boby's small group of five locals. This would provide a confidence booster for the local troops in Bubanja. As we drove into Bubanja it was dark and there was occasional mortar and machine gun fire but nothing heavy. The main problem was sniper fire; the Chetniks must have been using night scopes. We got to the HQ safely where John and I were immediately sent out to man a forward bunker which had been abandoned by the panicky locals. We took a local with us to show us where the bunker was. The local was obviously very edgy, and pointed it out to us from a distance of about 20 metres and then slithered off. Thankfully we had also been told before we left the HQ that Joe and Lars from the Ulice team had arrived earlier and had gone forward to set up a listening post to warn of any attack prior to our arrival, so we had to keep an eye out for them returning. John and I found the bunker and jumped in. As I watched the area to our front through the 'borrowed' portable, battery operated night scope I saw two figures approaching our position. I recognised Joe from his bushy beard; he said 'strasha' in a low voice, strasha is Croatian for friend or ally. I replied, 'come in Joe'. He seemed relieved to hear my voice; a 'gruff Lancashire drone' he called it. They had been a little worried about being fired on by the nervous local guard. Joe told me that they had heard noises ahead, but it was probably rabbits or a deer. We stayed in the bunker until we were relieved at 1:30am by Ron and Radek. I told them that the only action had been from random sniper fire, three rounds all fired in our direction, all hitting the trees above us. They may have been trying to draw our fire. I told them he was about 400-500 metres away and that he was a useless tosser or words to that effect.

As we made our way back to the HQ I had already realised that we had been called out for nothing, the locals had just got panicky. I certainly do not expect a dawn attack on Bubanja, however, we were back in the bunker by 5:30am, only to be relieved an hour after first light by the more confident local troops. Ten minutes later both teams and Bobys group were on our way back to Donji Vuksic for some sleep.

Tomorrow is the 1st of August; I had been here well over a month already! The run out date on my train ticket home is the 28th. Will I still be here? The shelling I could hear before going to bed that night seems to be getting closer, and I can also hear .50 calibre machine gun fire as the Serbian war machine gets closer to our own little village. The whole area we are operating in is slowly becoming encircled, a circle that seems to be getting smaller daily. We are now packing some of our equipment ready for a bug out. I always thought the good guys won, maybe I chose the wrong side.

I had to meet Boby at 10:00am the following morning. He is going to take John and myself into Gorni Rahic to collect a diesel pump for another truck we are going to get. Our old one is being claimed back today by its legal owners at Jagodnjak, on the way we managed to swap Johns PAP bolt action rifle and two hand grenades for another SSG Steyr sniper rifle identical to mine. We were back in Donji Vuksic by 5:00pm and gave the village mechanic the new second hand diesel pump; hopefully the truck will be ready for us tomorrow as we are not much of an immediate reaction team without one. The thought of us taking a casualty and having no transport to get him to medical aid is not a good one. The locals here don't mind us fighting on their behalf, yet we have to beg for transport and every litre of diesel. As we drove back through Ulice this afternoon Joe and Lars told me they were going home next week, they have had enough. I spent the rest of the evening sat around the fire outside our house discussing nothing with the rest of the lads. Tomorrow is another day with nothing planned. We were however supplied with more ammunition, grenades and a few mines, and I managed to scrounge three more 64mm LAWs, the new Russian version. All this ammunition is supposed to be held in reserve until we, that are the whole of 108 brigade, carry out the planned and planned and planned again assault on the main road to our north. This would cut the Serbian/Chetnik division who separate us from Croatia in half, leaving the eastern half without a supply line; it is a job I know could be done, although holding the road afterwards would be the problem. Weapons and ammunition are in short supply here and we would be up against armour, air strikes and heavy artillery. I did get some good news today, Pepi-Joe, one of the better locals is going back to Zagreb soon, and while he is there he is going to try and get a refund on my train ticket for me. He is also taking mail out if anybody in this strange bunch has got someone to write to - maybe which is why the locals call us the 'strangers'. Later in the afternoon we all opted for a swim in the natural pool formed by the river about 600metres north of here, it is only 10metres wide but it is 3m (9ft) deep. Before the war the local people used it a lot and there are diving platforms on the river banks. The only problem now is that the pool is on the edge of no-mans land and unprotected, if we do meet the enemy there, we will share the pool with them and shoot them later. We swam and dived into the pool for about two hours before the inevitable mud fight happened, we left after trying to wash ourselves down in the now filthy murky water. When we got back to our house Gaston, Nikolas and Francois had turned up; they had not bothered to join us for our bathing session. They were roasting a pig on our spit, as we realised we were about to host another barbeque. It seems the survival rate of the lesser and lesser spotted pig around here is not a good one. During the evening we ate and drank well, and talked about who and what was wrong with our work so Tom came in for a lot of stick. I felt quite sorry for him because I think that lately he has changed his attitude but a lot of it was still deserved. John fell asleep by the fire later, he is not yet used to the brandy and locally supplied Rakia, and being an ex-legionnaire he drank lots of it. He later woke up to find Dave had painted his head black which did not please him. He is a big lad, but for the moment all he can do is slur threats in Dave's direction. I went to my room in the early hours, locking the door behind me in case I woke up with a black head. I know I've had a few drinks but I seem to be thinking more of home; I wonder what I may have missed this weekend, a good time probably knowing the lads I hang around with back home. I think obviously of a certain woman and wonder if my dog Kafir is being looked after. It is probably because Joe and Lars have been discussing leaving for most of the evening, I also ask myself if we should really be here. I know I selfishly wanted my last fling at soldiering but I also saw this as helping a people defend themselves from attack by the last communist backed army in western Europe, but it was some of these same people I watched doing a Nazi salute whilst singing the other night. I am now feeling only committed to those I know I can trust, the Brits and other foreigners here and Boby's group of Croatian HVO troops.

I woke up eight hours later suffering slightly. It turns out that the reason Gaston arranged the barbeque last night was because he wants volunteers for an attack cum raiding party for tonight. I think I'll go back to bed; I can't handle a French plan and a hangover. Nikolas probably wants to bayonet charge a tank, Nikolas is always going on about fighting the Serbs with bayonets fixed, I am not in the slightest bit interested in getting that close. In fact if I ever come across a screaming Chetnik running at me with a fixed bayonet, I hope to have enough ammunition to shoot the idiot several times! In the end Gaston was informed by HQ that his plan had been knocked on the head, for tonight anyway. They would let him know more later 'maybe tomorrow'. By 1:00pm it was boiling hot so we decided to head for the pool again, minus our French friends. While we were up there John, who had come up to wash his black head, told us his story of his trip here. He had ridden from Paris where he was working in a bar, to Zagreb on a 49cc moped; the journey took him a week! I retired early that evening and went to bed, booze free, at 9:30pm. After a good 11 hour sleep I went outside to find Broadmoor's truck abandoned there, the keys are missing presumed lost in the pool and it has no diesel. The keys are no problem, I can cross the fuses to get the ignition on and it has a starter button, but until we can scrounge some diesel it will stay there.

Dave, our Vuksic team commander has been informed he now holds the rank of Captain, and is now the village second in command; all he has to do now is kill Boby and he then owns his own village in Bosnia! I am now a platoon advisor with Radek as my 2i/c, not that it means much, though it may look good on paper. They are trying to organise the villages into British army type companies, but it will take a lot more training and instruction than we can give them in the time we have. By 1:00pm it was time for a swim again, Joe, Lars and Andreas came with us before returning to Ulice. Gaston has gone to Dubrava for a recce in the hope of reviving his plan, he wanted two volunteers from our team to go with him, but until our own truck is repaired there is no transport, so he's going to hitch a lift or walk. I tried to get it into his head that it was not a good idea, but he was determined to go anyway. Ron went with him as did Radek who I don't think fully understands the situation.

Apart from the embarrassment of having to hitch lifts off the people we are supposed to be fighting for, I tried telling Gaston it would be too dangerous to go down onto the road without a back up team to give them covering fire should they run into trouble. Even worse, if they should take a casualty, how would they get him back to medical aid without transport? I will admit though, he doesn't lack anything in the courage department.

Later in the evening I sat outside with Tom and three local men from our village came to sit with us. In a conversation which was a mixture of broken English, German and Croat, they got onto the subject of why the Americans and Europeans are not helping them. They believe that the Americans and Europeans may be holding back because of their (Croatian) link to World War 2 Germany. They find this unfair because they consider themselves true Europeans; I told them that I thought the UN would be here soon. I was eventually right but they took their time about it. I soon got bored and left Tom to break down the language barrier by himself.

12.

I got up early the next morning; there was no sign of Gaston, or of our two, Ron and Radek, I hoped they were OK. It had rained hard during the night so I cleaned and oiled the mortar in its position. Dave had scrounged 10 litres of diesel from somewhere the night before so I decided to try and get Broadmoor's truck going, I put 5 litres of diesel into the tank then bled the system, crossed the fuses, did a slight re-wiring job, pressed the starter button and she spluttered into life. Now came the problem of the steering lock on the steering column which I decided to smash off. I was just delivering the final blow when the owner turned up with a spare set of keys with the intention of repossessing his truck. He took one look at the wiring hanging loose from the dashboard and the recently functional steering lock, and proceeded to throw a wobbler. I don't understand the language but I think I may have upset him! As it turns out Broadmoor had only borrowed it from him for a couple of hours which had been a week earlier. The owner said that if there had been any policemen here he would have him arrested for theft. I explained to him through a group of locals who had turned out to see the commotion, that I would give him his truck back tomorrow but we needed it today as we had two of our lads out somewhere with a mad Frenchman and we wanted it in case we had to go and get them. I also told him to bring his own diesel because this was mine, though I think in the end the only reason he agreed was the fact that I had a gun and he didn't.

That afternoon the remainder of our team (Dave, John, Tom and I) went for a drive into Polijaci to collect some more .308 ammunition for the sniper rifles. While we were there they invited us to stay for a meal. We arrived back in Donji Vuksic at 8:00pm. Boby met us, he had heard via the radio that Ron and Radek along with Gaston were OK and would be back tomorrow. He also said we would be getting a new truck for sure tomorrow. Obviously he had heard about today's events. In the morning I listened to the English speaking news at 8:00am on an old car radio I had rigged up to a truck battery. There was nothing much about our area, its quiet around here at the moment, but we are always being told to expect pushes which so far have not materialised. I spent the whole day doing practically nothing, washed some clothes and did an hour's physical training with John. It has been a week since we have been involved in anything constructive, or should I say destructive.

Our new truck arrived this evening; it's an old basic communist era truck. I drained our diesel out of the 'stolen' truck and added the other five litres into ours, and sent a message to Mr. Happy to come and get his. I checked our new truck over, it has two seats in the cab, a steering wheel, gear stick and speedometer, absolute basics, but if it gets us from A to B it will do.   Ron and Radek returned at 11:00pm. Not happy lads, Gaston's mission had been blocked by local commanders, I will find out more in the morning. I wound Radek up about him missing a slap up meal yesterday, to which; 'fuck off Steve', was his reply. I went to bed.

The next day started with nothing to do as usual. I made a fire for the morning brew and we sat and listened to the news on the radio. I spoke to Ron and Radek who were still not happy. They had spent two days being told OK go, no wait, go, wait, until they were finally refused permission by the Croat commander in Dubrava who feared repercussions from the Chetniks, e.g. a mortar attack on his base. I spent the rest of the day working on the new truck. I checked it over before painting camouflage markings all over it.   I also rolled up the side canvas to make it easier to get out of in the event of an ambush. When I'd finished John and I took the truck into Ulice to try to get some more diesel for it. When we found the man in charge of the diesel we were promptly refused despite explaining we needed it to carry out operations, I then lost my temper and threatened to empty the fat git's own diesel engined VW Golf which was probably full to the brim to help him to escape in case the Chetniks invaded. I also told him that I hoped they did invade because I would help them burn Ulice. Gaston heard the abuse and intervened, we eventually got 15 litres. On our return we went to join the others at the pool. Our new Captain Dave was there and he told me that soon we would be working in the village of Gorice to our north. It is supposed to be deserted but heavily patrolled by Chetniks. There were plenty of looks on faces that said we've heard it all before. On the walk back from the pool, Ron said that he thought that this Gorice trip had been thought up to prevent us going back to Brcko. The way the local commanders looked at it, was any ammunition used there, was ammunition we could use here in the event of an attack. The rest of the lads have been discussing leaving at the end of September, Joe and Lars who were going this week, have decided to stay on until then, so we can all leave together. Of course I have said I will go as well. That means I have 54 days left. We also found out that Dog, who had come back this morning after being out all night, had returned with three large gashes on him. Along with the other village dogs he had been tangling with a wild bear. John patched him up and he seems OK although I don't fancy the idea of bumping into a bear on a night patrol.

Up early next morning. Dave and I went into Jagodnjak and Ulice to get details of the future recce patrol in Gorice. Gaston's team at Ulice is to join us while Francois' group, minus Brale, who originally comes from Gorice, will be clearing a minefield between Markovic Polje and Lanista. Brale will be attached to us as a local scout. Both operations are scheduled for a 4:00am start tomorrow. In Ulice we managed to scrounge another 10 litres of diesel and get hold of a fully charged battery for our radio. 53 days to go. Up at 3:30am and sorted my kit for the patrol. After both teams had arrived and were briefed, we left by vehicle for our separate tasks.

I parked the truck about two kilometres south of Gorice just past Donji Rahic. We moved towards the village in darkness, on foot. Information had been given to us that the Chetniks were storing ammunition and explosives in a wood to the left of the village. Our team split up on the outskirts of the village, into a fire support group and a four man recce team. The recce team would move into the village centre to find out if it was occupied, if not then they would carry out a search of the wood while we waited in fire support. The recce team returned nearly an hour later, there wasn't as much material in the wood as was first thought. The team did manage to recover a box of explosives and some cortex explosive fuse wire. Once we had regrouped we made our way back to the vehicle and base, arriving back at 9:30am.

After breakfast (stew), I cleaned my AK-47 and the SSG Sniper rifle and went to bed until 4:00pm. That evening before we went up to the north position of our village for a pig roast we had been invited to, Boby came round and asked if he could have my opinion on the explosive find we had this morning. I went round to his house to check it out and my first impression was one of shock that the two Croats who carried it back were still with us. The explosive was plastic or semtex type material, and packed in wax papered rolls and each roll was of about a pound or half kilo in weight. There were approximately 25-30 pounds of the stuff, it was in a really poor condition, moist and very sticky looking. I told Boby that was probably why it had been dumped, where they had found it, along with the 200m of cortex fuse wire which looked no better. I told him if he was going to keep it, to put it in a dark cold storage room far from me. He wanted to know if it could be used but I told him he would have to get some detonators for it, to be possible to tell, then we could try out a small test, to know for sure. He thanked me and I left him alone to store it and made my way up to the pig roast.

Francois was there; he had recovered nine Serbian mines this morning and plans to resite them to our own advantage in the near future. We may be going back to Brcko on Tuesday and this time we are to take the 82mm mortar and thirty bombs for it, so we can expect a lot of retaliation. It may get very noisy. Dave wants me to give the rest of our team a run through on the mortar in the morning. Got up early again to catch the 8'o clock news, it was mainly the same old propaganda, although Osijek, the town I passed through on my way here, had been shelled during the night. Later in the morning I got Tom, Radek and John for some mortar instruction and we practised the setting up and firing drills prior to our Brcko trip in the morning. The lads picked it up easily and I think we all needed the training session. I spent the afternoon cleaning out my room and doing some washing. Some supplies had got through to us at last; we got coffee, sugar, soap, shampoo, toothpaste and even a new T-shirt each. When we went down for our evening meal (stew), we met Dave who had been into Ulice to scrounge some diesel; he told us that the Brcko trip was off. HQ would not authorise the diesel to get us there and back. I don't really understand why, but it was off, Dave has given us several reasons but it just seems to me that lately when we try to organise something against the Chetniks, we are held back. We can and would do the job so why won't they let us? They don't want us to go home, in fact far from it, but they don't want to let us fight either. Not yet anyway it seems. Morale among us foreigners is now getting low, especially Dave, Joe, Lars, and Ron.

In the evening Boby came round to see us and to have a chat, he unfortunately asked the wrong question, 'are you all going in September,' he got a unanimous YES! Not the answer I think he wanted to hear. Boby had brought round some Rakia, a village concoction that was supposed to be plum brandy. We sat around playing chess, talking and drinking Boby's Rakia. When I got Boby on his own I asked him if there was any news of Pepi-Joe's trip back to Zagreb as I still need the refund on my train ticket. He told me that Pepi-Joe did not yet know if he could sort it, but said I shouldn't worry about a fare home as we will all be paid our fares when we left. I told him that if I thought he would be responsible for our payment I would believe him, but as we must go back to the 'Club Brcko' for the money it was another matter. I do not want to get back and find there is no money and my ticket is out of date. I didn't come here for any wages but I would like help with my fare home, especially if I have stayed longer than I planned.

Up again at 7:00am, Dave and Boby have just been summoned to the HQ at Ulice. I found John and Tom lying next to the radio outside, where they had fallen asleep last night. I woke them up with a coffee, both look worse for wear, probably something to do with all the Rakia they drank last night. Later in the morning, Gaston and Nikolas came up from Ulice; they told us that they are to join us on an ambush planned for Gorice tomorrow. Dave and Boby will return later to give us a fuller briefing. Gaston also said that the Ulice team is being moved to Bijela. Joe, Lars and Andreas are moving today, and

Broadmoor wants to move here to carry on with the training of the locals. In the evening Dave and Boby returned, we got a semi-briefing, we know who's going, where we are going and when but the mission has not yet been decided. Boby does not want us to go into Gorice and set up an ambush, he fears repercussions on this village. He wants us to stay on the outskirts and snipe at targets.

Whatever happens we will more likely find out tomorrow, when we will go out half cocked, and if they hit us first, we will run around like headless chickens! Talking of chickens. Tom's pet chicken, which he swapped, whilst under the affluence of alcohol, for the M48 rifle he found on a search, has gone missing in action, he has been feeding it up for the past week and now that it has gone he wants to know who has eaten it! After the briefing we all went into Jagodnjak to eat with Francois' team. At 9pm with full bellies, Radek and I decided to set off walking and let the truck catch us up. We needed the exercise. In the half hour that we had been walking, and the truck picked us up, I found the plan had changed once more. We may now put an ambush on a cafe building in the centre of the village. I didn't really want to listen, I'll find out more 'maybe tomorrow'!

Up at 3am, got dressed and put a brew on for the lads, we left our house once all the group had arrived, at 4:30am. Our six man team, plus Gaston and Nikolas, plus four locals who were Mico and another on the MG42 Spandau 7.9mm machine gun and Pepi-Joe (now back from Zagreb, without my refund) plus Angelo, who would be our scouts. We drove up to the northern position, debussed and headed for Gorice on foot in single file, this time we would approach the deserted village from the west. Once on the village outskirts, we began our move into the centre, creeping slowly past the houses and through the overgrown gardens until we arrived at the deserted cafe/bar. Only then did I realise we would not be ambushing or hitting the cafe but setting up an ambush at the cafe. A hurried plan was issued and we set ourselves into position. I don't fully understand the plan, then again neither does anyone else it seems. Nothing like a good plan to let us know what the fuck is happening. The village does seem to be deserted though. The bar/cafe we had positioned ourselves in had been looted previously, what hadn't been stolen was strewn around the floor. According to local intelligence, what happens is that every morning between 8:00 and 8:30 a Chetnik pick up truck comes into Gorice from Krepsic, drives down the road and turns round outside the cafe. The vehicle contains four or five of the local Chetnik militia and they check that the village is deserted each morning. Ten o'clock came and I wasn't surprised when the vehicle hadn't turned up, so we bugged out once more without a result.

I have the feeling that our presence was known. Talking to Dave later about the patrol, I began to understand his problems. We sat here yesterday planning this patrol but it was changed twice during briefing by people who weren't even on the operation. I asked him why he hadn't flipped, and he said that he had been here for seven months and was used to doing things the 'Bosnian way' or roughly translated, 'off the cuff', something that any British ex-soldier will not get used to.

We arrived back at our house at 1:00pm after dropping the other teams off. I got my head down for a couple of hours after tea. Broadmoor was at the cookhouse when we arrived for our daily stew ration; he is apparently staying out of any military involvement and flatly refuses to get involved in any actions either now or in the future. He says he wants only to instruct, and stays inside the village perimeter, walking around with his two pistols, one shoulder holstered the other hanging from his belt, bartering and trying to do deals with the locals. I don't know what's wrong with him and he doesn't want to talk to me about it. I wonder if our close shave with the tank has upset him. The other lads are even questioning his previous military experience of 8 years in the Royal Artillery and 5 years French foreign legion.

13.

Got up the next morning and made a brew. There was nothing planned for today, but that changed with a 'move out in five minutes' call from Boby at 10:45am. A local patrol had bumped into a Chetnik patrol in Gorice where we had lain in wait yesterday. We jumped into the truck and drove straight to Donji Rahic where the patrol was from. When we eventually got there, we were too late as the Chetnik patrol had already withdrawn. A patrol of Bosnian troops from Donji Rahic had been on the southern outskirts of Gorice when they saw a Chetnik patrol coming towards them, they waited for them to get within 300metres before opening fire with an MG42 Spandau machine gun, only for it to jam after two rounds, (it was still jammed when they arrived back, and Radek fixed it for them). With the surprise lost, each side engaged each other as they both withdrew, neither knowing the others strength. Later we learned that the Chetnik patrol was seven strong, ours was six. The local group had one wounded and claimed that they had hit one Chetnik. We remained in position for an hour but were then told to return to Donji Vuksic by Boby who had come with us. On our return through Ulice, we met Gaston and Nikolas who asked Dave if they could have four of our team for an operation tonight at Dubrava. Dave said that myself, Tom, Radek and Ron could be spared, as he and John are going on a recce in Krepsic tonight with Pepi-Joe and Matia.

Things seem to be livening up around here at the moment, I wonder how long for? When we got back Dave asked me if I had changed my mind about wanting to use my ticket home on the 28th August. I told him I may have to leave earlier in time to get to Zagreb before the 28th unless we had more than just a promise of return fare. He's being a bit off with me at the moment, but like the lads say, we are all volunteers here and can leave when we choose, not when he chooses.

We left for Dubrava at 9:00pm, arriving at 11:00pm and I got my head down until 2:00am. The plan was for one team consisting of Joe, Lars, Andreas, Tom and two Croatians, Pelec and Tidi to fire at any vehicles on the main road as had been done previously. They would also act as a fire support team, for our team should we get into trouble. The second team of Gaston, Nikolas, Radek, Ron and I would move from the houses across no-man's land onto the road itself and position Claymore mines on the road and hit the vehicles directly from the roadside. Hoping the Chetniks would believe the fire to be coming from the other team in the houses still 500m away. Gaston would use the 'Striker', a six cylindered grenade (M79) launcher, and Nikolas would detonate the Claymores. Ron would take the RPG7 anti-tank weapon in case they brought out a tank or the 'Praga'. Myself and Radek would be one hundred metres from these ready to provide immediate fire support with our AK-47's. I also carried a 64mm LAW. We moved away from the church and HQ buildings and across the 700m of ground to the houses, from there we moved out into no-man's land in single file. It was a full moon so we stayed well into the tree line, as we moved alongside the left hand wood, so as to keep from being seen by the Chetnik sentries on the roads or in case they had any patrols of their own nearby. At around 5:00am, Radek and I were dropped at our position and we began the wait while the other three moved forward onto the roadside, also at this time the fire support team should have been moving into their positions around the houses to our rear. An hour later I lay in the tree line facing the road on which we were to fire if need be, suddenly, I heard slow shuffling noises coming straight towards us through the woods. I looked at Radek next to me, who had also heard it; we both slipped off our safety catches and lay still. It was just becoming light as dawn broke. The shuffling noise got closer and closer, it started to sound as though at least two people were moving slowly towards us, quite possibly a Chetnik clearance patrol. As the steps got nearer, we could hear the undergrowth snapping and twigs breaking. My poor old heart was pounding as the steps got closer towards us, as we had both tensed up, fingers on triggers, lying deadly still when suddenly out of the undergrowth six feet away, we looked directly into the eyes of a deer which saw us and sprinted away. I looked at Radek, rolled my eyes and smiled coolly but it must have taken five minutes before my heart was beating normally again. At around 7:00am the next shock came as a tank started its engines, to our left in front of us, no more than 100 metres away probably parked on the roadside. It ran its engines for about five minutes and then cut them; obviously it was in a static position and could prove to be a danger to us if we are caught here, 500m from our lines. I was beginning to seriously wonder if I've got the stomach for this job as I lay silently listening to the clanks and thumps coming from the parked tank's position as the crew got themselves up, only two hundred metres away. It was agreed that we would only fire on vehicles coming from Pelagicevo as these would most likely be carrying men and supplies to Cerik, the first vehicle was a jeep coming from Cerik so we let it be. An hour later the jeep returned, this time coming from Pelagicevo. The fire support group to our rear opened fire from their positions before the vehicle came into view, as planned, to cover the noise of our group. I knelt up and fired a burst of 8-10 rounds from my AK, at the same time I saw Gaston's striker grenade, hit the embankment above the vehicle and explode. I don't know how many, or if any of the rounds I fired, hit the vehicle as it sped by, as my position was still 100m from the road. Once the vehicle had sped past the gap I could hear it braking rapidly as it came to a halt. By now, the fire support team had ceased firing so we got back down into the undergrowth to wait and see what the Chetnik reaction would be. From my position, I could hear the vehicle doors slamming and shouting coming from the road.

The two machine gun positions in the Chetnik bunkers on the main road opened up simultaneously. At first, as the rounds cracked above us, I stuck my face into the ground but then realised the cracks the rounds made as they passed above us were high. I looked up and behind to see the tracer rounds bouncing off the buildings belonging to the fire support team 500m away. They were taking it for us, hopefully our plan was working. The Chetniks did not yet realise our group was right in front of them. Gusts of smoke reeking of cordite were now wafting over the position held by Radek and myself as the left hand machine gunner hammered round after round towards the houses, hopefully our fire support team was safely inside their bunkers. A second vehicle had now arrived from Cerik and stopped roughly in the same position that the jeep had come to a halt. I could hear all this going on but I couldn't see through the trees. Minutes later it turned around and drove back in the direction of Cerik, after another minute the firing died down and then ceased. Gaston caught my eye and told me to stay in position by way of hand signals, obviously we were not going to withdraw yet. He wanted to Claymore the next vehicle that passed, the Claymore mines would be detonated remotely by wires, by Nikolas, who had set two up earlier on the roadside, under the cover of darkness. These mines were of Soviet manufacture but were an exact replica of the American or NATO mines used by the west. Earlier, Nikolas had crawled up to the road and placed two mines at the base of two trees with the front of the mine facing onto the road. Each mine when detonated electrically by Nikolas, would fire a thousand ball bearings across the road. We settled in to wait once more. It seemed like hours passed as I lay in the undergrowth next to Radek, trying to listen for the slightest noise, although I knew it must be worse for Gaston, Nikolas and Ron in their position 10 metres from the roadside, the silence was broken twice by the nervous Chetniks in their bunkers, who twice fired about fifty rounds above us towards the houses, both times I worried that Gaston's small group had been discovered. Sometimes we heard the Chetniks talking and shouting to one another. Then we all heard another approaching engine noise as a vehicle sped down the road towards us from the right. The fire support team began firing onto the road, the rounds cracking above us as they headed for the road. I knelt up, as did Radek, put the butt in my shoulder and sighted on the road, suddenly a black pickup truck doing about 50mph came into view with five or six camouflaged figures crouching in the back. I aimed in front of the vehicle and emptied the magazine of the twenty or so rounds I had left into the pick up. The sound of Radek firing next to me was making me go deaf in my left ear. The vehicle went into the tree line from where I heard the sound of Nikolas' Claymores detonating; I got back down and changed my magazines. My left ear was ringing loudly but I could still hear the pickup rolling along the road, the only sound now though was a sort of flapping noise, probably one or more shredded tyres, but there was no sound of an engine. It then rolled into the banking with a crunch and then heard lots of screaming and shouting from the roadside. Then both bunkers opened up with machine guns as I stuck my head back in the ground again.

A couple of minutes later I saw Gaston approaching followed by the other two, he signalled to us to tag on with a broad smile on his face. The gunners were still firing above us in the direction of the fire support team, tracer rounds were bouncing off the ground around their houses, then came the familiar plops of mortar bombs leaving the tubes as we made our way cautiously back to our lines. The Chetniks still didn't seem to know that it was us right in front of them; they must have thought that the Claymores were rockets fired from the houses. The mortar rounds began impacting around the houses, eight rounds in all exploded all around the support team and we had a grandstand view. As the firing slowed and finally stopped we pressed on to our lines, as we made our way up the embankment I looked back and I could see the smoke from our Claymores still hanging in the air.

It was 11:45am when we got back to our lines, we had only been in position for seven hours but it seemed a lot longer. We were then greeted by the support team and we thanked them for taking the gun and mortar fire which should have been ours, Tom confirmed that the pickup truck had been hit by the two

Claymores. Before we trooped back we came under fire from the Praga again, the church tower took several direct hits from the 50mm cannon shells. According to the locals this was a sure sign that we had hurt the Chetniks, it seems that every time we come to Dubrava the church gets some. When we got back to the church the Praga fire had stopped and some of the locals had come out to survey the damage. As we were heading off towards Bijela I looked at the locals looking at their once more smoking church and wondered what they thought of us now - heroes, or villains? We dropped off Gaston, Nikolas, Joe, Lars, Andreas and the two Croatians at their new base in Bijela where we scrounged another 15 litres of diesel before setting off back to Donji Vuksic.

On our arrival back at the house I found a message from Boby asking to see me, but first I needed a shower and some sleep. I got up and went for some stew at 6:30pm. Gaston had asked for us to go back to Dubrava early tomorrow morning to repeat the action but I can't say I will definitely go until I know what Boby wants. John has volunteered to go in my place. He hasn't seen any action yet but he wants to of course. In the evening the rest of our team went to a pig roast. I declined the invitation because I had to see Boby and I'm sick of pig lately.

I found Boby outside his house along with Pepi-Joe, Angelo and Vinko who had come in the supply van from the 'Club Brcko'. Vinko is the secretary of the Club Brcko in Zagreb, our employers, I suppose. Boby told me that if I really had to leave I could return tomorrow with Vinko, but he also said that he would prefer it if I stayed, Vinko said he would take my ticket and get a refund for me or get me a new ticket, he would then send the money or the ticket back on the next convoy from Zagreb. I told Boby that if he was absolutely sure this would be done then I would stay, if my ticket problem had been sorted I am willing to stay, firstly because I don't want to be the first one to leave the team, I'd rather we all left together in September, and secondly, I don't feel as if I have finished just yet!

Back at the house I found the team had just returned from Jagodnjak, the pig roast was cancelled until tomorrow because the Jagodnjak team was working tonight. I told them about my talk with Boby and also that Vinko would take any mail for posting back to England. I was woken by Ron at 3:00am. He, Radek, Tom and John were going to Dubrava to repeat the action but they couldn't wake John, he had got pissed with Dave somewhere last night and was out of it.

I wasn't supposed to be on this operation, but I am now. I quickly dressed, grabbed my AK and had a quick cup of coffee before we left for Dubrava. Ron quickly filled me in on this mornings plan: Gaston and Nikolas would go down onto the road again, open fire at short range at the first vehicle to pass and then bug out immediately. Radek and Tom would provide immediate fire support should they need it from the position I was in yesterday. Ron and I would fire in support from the houses. Only six of us out this morning. We arrived at Dubrava at 4:00am. Ron and I were in our bunker position near an old combine harvester by the houses by 4:30am, and at exactly 6:00am we started firing at the two bunker positions to let them know we were here, and to lead them into thinking the only threat was again from our position. It must have worked because at 7:15 a jeep came screaming down the main road. Gaston and Nikolas fired directly into it as it sped by from a distance of 10m, it crashed to a halt 100m up the road. Ron and I then began firing from our position once more while Gaston and Nikolas collected Tom and Radek and made their way back to our position which by now was receiving machine gun fire. Then came the familiar 'plops' as mortar bombs arched their way towards us. We got down in the bunker to await their arrival, as I lay there I remember thinking; 'when haven't I been shelled?' I have only been here for a couple of months and already the idea of being shot at, shelled or mortared was becoming a mere routine. By the time the other four had made their way to our position all the firing had died down. Six mortars had exploded to the right of our position, one of them hitting the right hand building but this was damaged and in danger of falling down anyway.

We made our way back to the church and Dubrava HQ for a quick debrief. Gaston and Nikolas had both fired about twenty rounds into the jeep, plus our contribution when it crashed, which at 500 metres can't have been much. It wasn't known how many were in it, possibly three but nobody was seen to get out. Before heading back to Donji Vuksic we had breakfast in the Dubrava canteen. We arrived back at 10:00, had a quick wash to get rid of the camouflage cream and dived into bed. I was woke once more at 3:30pm by Dave who was pissed again, he was trying to round everyone up to go to the promised pig roast at Jagodnjak. How does he get in that state and where does he get it all from? I once more declined the offer and went out into the garden to strip and clean my AK. I washed some clothes and then sat down to catch up on the diary I am keeping.

The team came back from Jagodnjak later in the evening, some of them a little worse for wear, except Radek who doesn't drink. Dave was a complete mess, maybe the job of being commander is getting to him, he has been here a lot longer than the rest of us, and since he heard the news of his friend Milo's death in captivity, he's been hitting the drink in a big way! If he doesn't have a BIG hangover tomorrow, there's no justice in the world. Radek has brought me a bottle of beer back. I'll enjoy it while reading one of Ron's books - Hyena Dawn - Cheers Radek! Today I should have, or could have been leaving this country. Whether I'll regret my decision only time will tell, I hope I don't.

14.

I was up at 6:00am as I couldn't sleep so went outside and made a brew. Radek was also up, same problem; we had a few coffees and a game of chess. Ron and Nikolas appeared later with some corn on the cob, but I think they will be in bed before they are cooked; they've been out all night on the pop and look rough.

Preparing for a pig roast.

I can't wait to see the other heads as they rise, there should be some thick ones. I'm glad I didn't go last night - the glee of being sober, amongst drunks!

Today's a day off up to now so I'll dig out my room, do some more washing and then inspect the heads as they appear. In the evening we were invited to another pig roast at the north position of our village. As it's Sunday I'm going because the cookhouse here is closed on Sunday evenings, plus we are going to be briefed on the way up about an ambush patrol in Gorice again, early tomorrow. At the briefing we got news that the Pickup truck ambushed at Dubrava on Friday had resulted in three kills and two wounded. In retaliation the Chetniks mortared the town of Bijela with over 50 mortars hitting the town. They hit at civilians to get back at us, there was a lot of damage but thankfully no civilians killed. We'll pay them back one day; maybe tomorrow.

Up at 3:30am and woke the team plus Gaston and Nikolas who had stayed overnight, got dressed, donned the 'cam cream' and left here at 4am to link up with the Croats who were coming with us. Surprisingly, Broadmoor is coming with us as well, he has told Dave that he wants to start working with us again, I don't know how long it will last but I honestly hope he sticks it out. After coffee at the northern position, we set out in single file cross country to Gorice. We arrived there an hour later, unchallenged, and moved slowly once more into the centre of the village and set up an ambush position around the Cafe -Bar. I noticed that dog had come along as well; he must have followed us out. We made safe the booby traps left behind on our previous visit, which were untouched and settled in to wait once more. After we had been in position for about two hours, I was watching up the road through my sniper scope when I saw the tint of a windscreen flash in the early sun and then I watched the back of a jeep flash past about 400 metres away. The jeep had been in the background of a road, crossing the one we were to ambush. I watched the area for a few more minutes but saw no more movement and I let Dave know what I had seen as we settled in to wait once more. Should the vehicle approach, the plan was for me to initiate the ambush by signalling to Nikolas, who would detonate the two Claymore mines that we had set up earlier, after five minutes though, nothing had showed or could be heard apart from a flock of birds that had been disturbed by someone or something moving ahead. I went forward and observed the road through the sniper scope, I immediately saw a Chetnik soldier looking around the front of a house for about three seconds, before he ran back to the area where I had last seen the jeep. I thought about firing at him but couldn't as I would have been giving the ambush position. I again let Dave know what I had seen and he thought it was best to stay in position and wait to see if they are tempted, to come any closer down our road. After another 30 minutes, Gaston and Dave decided on taking a small group forward to see what the Chetniks were doing. Gorice is a deserted village but is mainly in Chetnik held territory and they feel confident enough to carry out 'shopping' trips during the day. Shopping is the loose term for the looting of the unoccupied houses. Dave, Gaston, Pepi-Joe and Broadmoor were to go forward along with Ron and I who were both equipped with a sniper rifle. We moved along the hedgerows and roadside ditches for 250 metres from the ambush position, where Ron and I were dropped off to cover the team's move further along the road to spot and cover any possible Chetnik sniper positions. The other four moved slowly forward to the position where I had seen the Chetnik soldier. They came back forty-five minutes later to say that they had seen two or three leaving the village at the north end carrying their sacks of booty, which they had stolen from the houses. It was decided to go back and join the rest of the team and wrap up the ambush. We had missed them again.

Once the mines had been made safe and collected, we covered all traces of our visit, leaving no booby traps this time. We set off across country complete with Dog for Donji Vuksic. We had only got 800metres outside of the village, when we all had to jump into cover as a JNA (Yugoslav National Army) Serbian military Gazelle helicopter, flew past and on a parallel with us about 500 metres away. Definitely not a UN Chopper which would be white, this one was painted green but it was definitely a Gazelle which I only thought was used by the west or NATO countries. It would have been nice to have a blast at it but we wanted to remain unseen as we will return to re-ambush Gorice in the near future. Got back to Donji Vuksic at midday, had a brew, washed off the cam cream that had not come off with sweat and went to bed. Got up later at 5:30pm and went for some stew, after a drink at Broadmoor's. He's 35 today. Old bastard!

I've just been thinking about the Gazelle that I saw today and wished that we had some. In fact, I wouldn't mind their air force, like the MIG's they use, although we haven't had the pleasure of them yet. They have tanks, artillery, mortars, vehicles and endless supplies of ammunition for their troops, why is it always us who are doing the probing and attacking? The largest piece of equipment we have is the single 82mm mortar of which I am the supposed operator, yet I have never even fired one. We have a couple of run down trucks but little diesel. Many of the locals carry bolt-action rifles or shotguns. John, as well as his sniper rifle is still carrying a Thompson 9mm sub-machine gun from the Second World War. We have a few light anti-tank weapons and grenades. The Chetniks should really be walking all over us. Maybe they will at some point.

We got news today about Saturday mornings ambush on the jeep. All six occupants of the jeep had been killed. SIX! That's nine in two days. They were unlucky, possibly stupid, or over confident and they died for it. Bijela was mortared again on Saturday night/Sunday morning, the strange thing is that Bijela was a town with a Serbian majority before the war. The Chetniks are destroying their own people's houses, two civilians died. Nothing was planned for the next day. I modified the shower barrel with an on/off barrel tap I found in Gorice yesterday. Did some washing, sunbathed and read my book. A good day off.

Boby came around to our house early the next day. He wants me to train a couple of his guys on the mortar this morning, Dave and Tom came too. We went up near the village of Drenova and set it upon targets we were in range of. I let them know all I know about the thing which isn't much, just what I can remember from the familiarisation course on the similar 81mm mortar I did in the British army. At least they know how to set it up and lay it on to targets, and now, like me, all they lack is practical experience. We did ask to use it but were refused.

Ron and John have gone on a recce back to Dubrava, they should be back tomorrow, they along with Gaston and Nikolas are going to find out if we can get two teams in close enough to destroy the two roadside machine gun bunkers with grenades, if not both, then maybe just one. We hope this might demoralise the Chetniks sufficiently for them to refuse to man their bunkers for fear of our attacks. We know they are already nervous as when we have been in or near their areas we have heard them shooting at shadows in the dark. The other day Joe, Lars and Andreas with some Croatians from Bijela attacked another roadside bunker with rifle fire. One of the two Chetnik guards who had got out to take a leak was killed and his mate ran off into the trees, followed by a hail of fire knowing Joe, Lars and Andreas. What surprised them was that the occupants of the bunkers 250m either side of the one they attacked ran away as well, they thought they would just take a shot at someone taking a pee and then ended up controlling one of their roads for a while. So when our lads get back we'll work out if it's possible to destroy the bunkers taking minimal risks. With forty-two days to go, this is not the time to start taking casualties.

In the evening Boby came round to ask us to go and look at his new toy, it was an old British 1950's 14.5mm anti-aircraft gun. Unfortunately none of us had even seen one before, let alone knew how to use it. He said the instruction book had come with it and was written in English but it turned out to be an armourer's defect report booklet. I couldn't help him, though you have got to wonder where the hell they got it from. Another day with nothing planned as yet, although we expect Ron and John back soon from their recce in Dubrava. Then we'll know if we are going to be out tonight or early tomorrow morning. Until then Tom and I will be instructing a crew of locals on the 82mm mortar so that they will have a trained crew for it when we leave in forty-one days. Ron and John got back at 2:00pm. They have found what they believe is a secure route to the right hand bunker on the road at Dubrava. We will be leaving at 6:30pm to liaise and plan the operation with the group there. After we had finished the training I prepared my kit for tonight's operation. I won't need the sniper rifle so I will carry a 64mm LAW in its place as well as my AK-47.

We left our house at 6:00pm, had some stew and then set off for Bijela. On arrival we went straight into the briefing room, where Broadmoor was in there on crutches. Apparently he had jumped off a bridge into a river yesterday when he was shot at and sprained his ankle, so he's off this one. In the briefing room we were told that the operation will take place early in the morning and will be for two groups. Joe and Lars will lead a team of Croatians and cause a diversion on the road between Cerik and Bijela at 7:00am. Our team, plus some locals, will move down on to the road, and just after 7:00am hit the right hand bunker with M79 grenades from Gaston's 'Striker'. Then we'll storm the bunker, kill or capture the occupants, take the weapons, set a booby trap in the bunker and then leave. Before leaving the briefing room we had a look at the local's mascot, a full size skeleton dressed in a black cloak and hood and carrying a scythe - The Grim Reaper! Not exactly a cheerful mascot, especially when you have to go out and face whatever.

After the briefing we all trooped up to Joe's new house he had occupied in Bijela to look at his electricity, running from a small farm generator. We all had a go of the light switch to remind us what it was - Electrickery! We also had a go of his taps with running water coming out of them; one of them even had HOT water coming out of it. In Donji Vuksic we only have a candle ration and well water. I didn't use their toilet, the flushing noise when you pulled the chain was unnerving and the paper was far too soft to write on. At 9:00pm Joe and Lars went to brief the Croatians who would be working with us, although the actual target was to be kept from them. We stayed behind to drink their Rakia - only a nightcap to help us sleep of course.

Joe and Lars returned an hour later to tell us that not one Croatian had turned up. A loud warning bell went off in my head; do they know something that we don't? I went back to the briefing room later with John and Dave to sleep. I said goodnight to the Grim Reaper in the corner and got my head down for a couple of hours. To be woken up at 3:00am. The first thing I focused on was the Grim Reaper. I didn't say good morning to him because I was beginning to get a bad feeling about this patrol especially as this was the third time we had hit the same stretch of road.

'Present Arms' with the Grim Reaper at Bijela

We had a coffee and both teams wished each other luck before setting off, minus our Croatian partners from Bijela. Joe and Lars were to carry out the diversion by themselves now, they were taking two LAW's each and they promised to make a lot of noise for the diversion. We arrived at Dubrava at 4:30am and made our way across the 700 meters of open ground to the houses waking up the sentries on the way to let them know that we were working in the area in front of them. All three sentry posts, each with two or three locals inside, had let us walk right up to them and had to be woken by our team! We moved across the open ground to the right hand wood and waited for first light before moving down to the road, rather than blundering through the wood in the dark and making enough noise to wake the dead. Our six man Donji Vuksic team and the three from the Bijela team made our way slowly in single file towards the road 300 metres away using the dry river bed and ditches as much as possible. At 6:10 am, just as the front end of the file reached the final RV, only 20 metres from the road in an open area of trees all hell broke loose. The left hand bunker started to fire at us with its machine gun, closely followed by the Chetnik right hand bunker. We all dived for cover as we realised we were caught in cross-fire, the rounds zipping around among the trees, I could clearly hear the Chetniks shouting orders to each other on the road. John and Nikolas, the second and third men in the file behind Gaston, managed to return fire to the left hand bunker while Gaston fired two M79 grenades from the striker. Between them they caused a casualty on the road who fell down and promptly started screaming obscenities, two rifle grenades then exploded in our confined area. Our patrol had been compromised in no uncertain terms, Dave realised very correctly that it was time to get out and quick. We had gone to ground in the 'killing area'. He signalled us to bug out, which the front men did, without hesitation. Rifle fire had now joined in with the machine gunners. The woods were buzzing with incoming and ricocheting bullets.

I was not in as bad a position as those at the front. I was the seventh member of the well spaced out patrol. I knew there was a ditch 50 metres to our rear which would offer us some protection. I called to Tom and Radek, who were behind me, to follow me as I set off at what felt like 100mph towards it just ahead of the stampeding front men. I jumped into the ditch closely followed by Tom and Radek and shouted to the others to join us. Less than a minute later the nine of us, now all accounted for, were in the ditch. We then decided to move back to another ditch which led on to the main dry river bed another 80 metres to our rear and out of the line of fire. We went for the second ditch, pushing through branches and smashing them out of the way, it felt like each obstacle was doing it's best to hold you back; each item of equipment was heavier than before. We all got into the ditch, safe but breathless. Now though the Praga had come out of hiding and had joined in the melee, its 50mm shells tearing through and exploding on the trees sending small pieces of shrapnel zipping through the air. It was 6:20am and from our position in the ditch we could hear the sounds of Chetnik reinforcements arriving in armoured personnel vehicles. It was only ten minutes since the first shot had been fired. Whoever these guys were, they were no fools, and the response had been too good, too quick. They certainly weren't two half asleep sentries in a bunker. The fire was beginning to dwindle and we could hear orders being shouted to the debussing troops. Fearing a follow up we began to pull back into the tree line and away from the road until we reached the dry river bed, here we waited and listened for movement behind us, as sporadic incoming fire still searched for us. None came, so we moved stealthily onto the hillside and back toward our lines.

As we made our way in single file through our lines the Croat guards came out to watch us pass, they seemed amazed that we had come out of the woods not carrying any wounded or dead. They had a grandstand view of our predicament from their positions above us, and heard and seen the amount of fire put down at us. I looked back at the woods, with the smoke from the explosions hanging above them and thought to myself, 'Lucky lads, all of us'. We plodded on to the church HQ. At the HQ buildings all the guard were stood outside as we came in. We laughed and called out to those we knew, trying on the 'didn't worry us' attitude as we boarded the truck and headed off to Bijela for the debrief and some breakfast.

At the debrief Drago, the Bijela HVO commander came in for some serious questions. We had all been thinking the same thing – this had been a set up! We wanted to know how they seemed to know of our arrival. Why did no Croatians turn up for this outing? If the Chetniks had been tipped off, how? Were we informed on? Had our mission been discussed on the radio, and if so, who by? We listen to the Chetnik transmissions, they must listen to ours. Drago tried to calm us down by saying he would find out and that they must improve their airwave security. He also said he would find out why the Croats were absent, one reason for this could have been the message from intelligence that we should have received yesterday. They believe that the Chetniks have been reinforced by a Serbian JNA Special Forces unit; 'The Tigers' from the regular army of about thirty men or platoon strength. Whether it was a language or communication cock up we don't know, but we never got that message, he said he would look into that as well. Even if there is this unit, that still didn't answer our questions. They had been waiting! We had been caught in a planned ambush, and we had been very lucky! We got back to Donji Vuksic at 12:30pm. After a quick wash I got my head down for a few hours. Just before I went to sleep I thought about this morning, if they'd really wanted to they could, or should have killed, wounded, or worse, captured us. Why hadn't they followed up? Did they know who we were ? How did they know?

Later in the evening I went to the cookhouse for my stew ration and then to the briefing arranged at Boby's. News is, the local garrison is pushing the line forward tomorrow. Thanks to our aggressive patrolling, no-man's land is dominated by us. The garrison is to take advantage and the line is to be pushed out all round early tomorrow, they will also set up static positions in the local unmanned villages between us and the Chetnik line.

The villages of Drenova and Lanista are to be permanently manned by Croatian troops. We, the 'foreigners' or 'strangers' are to go back to Dubrava again and keep the Chetniks busy until the task is completed. Oh well, they didn't kill us off today - maybe tomorrow.

15.

Up at 4:15am. The alarm was set for 4:00 but didn't go off; I only woke up by chance. I woke the team and lit a fire for the coffee. The two Croats from our village coming with us today turned up, they are Mico and his number two on the old Spandau machine gun. We set off for Bijela on time at 5:00am, picked up Gaston's team of Nikolas, Joe, Lars and Andreas and arrived at Dubrava for 6:30am.

Our job today was to stop traffic using the main road while the local Croatians push up the line. We must stop the town of Cerik getting supplies or ammunition this morning. The idea, as far as I understand it, is to keep the Chetniks busy trying to keep their supply road open so that our local forces can push forward and strengthen our area. During the next week we must make it difficult, or preferably impossible for Cerik to get supplies by hitting the road in several places and cutting it. This will stretch Cerik's forces to the limit because they can't be everywhere on the road at once, then in the future will come the taking of Cerik, the town is nothing special but it opens up a supply route for ourselves. Instead of transporting goods overland they can come to us, the Croatian HVO forces, and the Bosnian BIH Army by road. That's the plan anyway, so this morning we will cut the road from 7:00 to 11:00am to start with.

We set off in small groups from the church HQ so as not to alert the Chetniks. Joe Lars and I were to leave first. Our group was to be the RPG rocket team. We made our way across the open ground to the houses, once there I looked back to see the second group just about to cross the open ground, so we moved down to the dry river bed below. We positioned ourselves in the river bed facing the 500 metres of open ground just on the edge of the tree line, facing onto the road. As we were taking the rockets from their carrier pack and setting up our equipment we heard the engine of an armoured vehicle, we knew we could only observe because the others were not yet in their positions. An armoured transporter went across the road from right to left, closely followed by a coach full of JNA soldiers. What a target! Unfortunately all we could do was watch. We settled into our position in the river bed to wait. As we had no radio contact with each other we had to assume that everyone was in place at 7:00am which was our starting time. In the houses were Gaston and his group with the BST anti-tank cannon which fired RPG 9 rockets. Tom, Radek, and Ron would have the OSSA anti-tank launcher, a weapon similar to the NATO 84mm Carl Gustav but a lot lighter. Also in a separate position was the Croatian team with the MG42 Spandau machine gun. A lot of fire power, on our side for once. By 8:00am nothing more had passed on the road so Gaston came down and told us that we were all going to fire at the left hand bunker in fifteen minutes. Their gunner had been firing at the houses in long bursts, not hitting anything but making a real nuisance of himself. With any luck it will get them out on the road to retaliate, in other words, there isn't any trouble so we will start some. The problems started at 8:15 when Gaston's BST failed to fire, this was the signal to start firing so he shouted to Tom to fire the OSSA which he did, and then the Spandau joined in. Lars jumped up with the RPG 7, sighted on the bunker and fired

- nothing. He re-cocked the weapon and fired again, still nothing. He jumped back into the river bed to sort out his stoppage while Joe and I emptied a full magazine of thirty rounds each in the direction of the bunker from our AK's, which at a range of 500 metres was of little or no effect. I could see tracer rounds from the Spandau going into the bunker but I didn't see or hear the strike or explosion from the OSSA. My magazine empty, I jumped back into the river bed to change magazines and help Lars with the RPG 7. The percussion cap on the rocket's propellant igniter had only been lightly struck by the firing pin so we replaced the rocket, pushing it firmly into place. Lars jumped back up and tried again - click, still nothing. He re-cocked, pulled the trigger again and Whoosh! This time the rocket sped on its way and seconds later exploded in the area of the bunker. There was no response, either the two Chetniks had decided to keep their heads down or they had bugged out. The right hand bunker had obviously seen us though because very heavy 7.9mm rounds began shooting into the trees above us, from the river bank, all we could do was lay low in the river bed and watch the trees splinter above us as the rounds hit them. Watching this I made a mental note to find better cover in future, the heavy 7.9mm rounds would penetrate at least six inches into the trees, going straight through the smaller trunks. After a few minutes the firing died down, we re-checked the launcher as it was my turn to fire it. Great, I thought, I get to fire it when the machine gunner knows where we are. I checked my watch, 8:30, two and a half hours to go until bug out time. After another thirty minutes I was getting fidgety so I checked over the RPG again. The firing pin was worn but we didn't have a spare so it would have to do, I replaced the rocket, pushing it firmly into the launcher. The distinct noise of a transporter APC came across to us, I got up on the bank and settled into a kneeling position with the launcher on my shoulder sighted on the road. The transporter came into view moving fast from left to right, I sighted just in front of the vehicle and fired - click! I swore loudly and re-cocked the mechanism, the transporter was now moving towards the trees. I could hear the Spandau team firing at it and I heard Tom fire the OSSA but I saw the rocket disintegrate on the roadside without exploding, I sighted and squeezed the trigger again - click! Fuck it, I said, and scrambled back into the dry river bed to check the rocket. The percussion cap had been struck, so the rocket was a dud! I pushed it over the edge of the river bank. Ten minutes later when the incoming fire had died down once more, Gaston came down to ask us what our problem was, so I told him. He said that the BST had failed as well, also both Tom's rockets had failed to explode and the Spandau team had run out of ammunition. He decided it would be better for us to go up and join them at the bunker positions, it sounded like a good idea to me. We would have to use small arms and LAWs to stop traffic on the road. In the event nothing ventured back onto the road, and at 11:00am we prepared to move back, again in our small groups. This time our group would leave last.

The first group crossed the open ground safely, closely followed by the second group. Then as Toms group started to cross, the Chetnik sniper and his friends started up by putting a few rounds down, forcing Toms team to sprint or crawl across the remaining open ground. We set off too, to the sound of three mortars leaving their tubes, heading in our direction. We ran as fast as we could, knowing that the mortar bombs would be impacting within forty seconds. This was not easy for those carrying the heavier anti-tank weapons. As the first incoming mortar rushed in, swishing through the air, we threw ourselves to the ground, panting and heaving in the heat. Three bombs exploded on the ground, showering us with soil, I tried to pull my helmet down over my body, after the third impact it was time to move again, after first quickly checking that everyone was OK. Three more bombs left their tubes, the now familiar 'plops', an early warning. I remember running across the open ground as fast as my legs would go, and hearing the cracks of high velocity rounds passing through the air, fired by the Chetnik shooters on the road but not caring, just running, panting and trying to hear the swishing noise made by the incoming mortar bombs. I saw Radek go down so I followed him a second later, the three mortars exploded in the same area as before, now 200 metres away. I dragged myself up and ran towards the HQ buildings and flopped down, knackered and breathing heavily. A minute later Radek sauntered up and said with a big smile 'you OK Steve?' I told him what I thought, which was I'm 35 and far too old for this shit! He walked off laughing. Radek is 21, does not smoke or drink. Thankfully the rest of our group is around my age and just as fucked as me, or worse! After a few minutes of much needed recuperation, we picked ourselves up and went to find our truck. Once loaded and the evil fags lit up, we set off towards Bijela and breakfast. At 1pm, we left the Bijela team and set off back towards Donji Vuksic. Our crazy Czech Radek was still taking the Mickey out of us old folk in his broken English, 'Old men smoking is no good' He got a unified 'fuck off you Czech bastard!' He has now learned and understands these words well. I did not tell him that although I kept up with him crossing the open ground, I didn't hear the second volley of mortars coming in, because of my panting. I only hit the deck because I saw him go down. The others went down because we did. So he is of some use to us, it's a good job I like him!

Back at Donji Vuksic we were greeted by Dog, then some bad news. Francois' group had been operating in Gradacac yesterday. On one occasion of them being mortared, Brale had stepped out of his shelter, believing the fire had ended, when the last incoming mortar exploded twenty metres from him. A piece of shrapnel hit him in the forehead, just below the base of his helmet and went out of the back of his head. He died in Francois arms. He was a good bloke, a Croat who had left this area before the war and settled in Austria, he came back to fight for his local area and has now been killed for it. He had a wife and small child in Austria, I liked the guy, and he was one of the really decent Croatians. In the time I got to know him, he was always smiling, always helpful, and spoke good English.

He was with us a month earlier in the Brcko battle, and our scout in Gorice recently, I respected and liked him and I am sad at his loss. Francois is gutted. The funeral is to be held at Donji Rahic tomorrow.

That next morning I got up and cleaned my uniform and boots for the funeral at 10:00am. When the whole team was ready, we drove out to Donji Rahic. It was a good funeral for Brale, many people came from the outlying villages, especially from Jagodnjak where he had been based. It was the first funeral that I had been to here, and different than to what I am used to. The coffin is sealed at the graveside and candles are lit and left to burn on the grave. I hope it is the last funeral I have to attend and I also hope Brale's death was not a waste.

I spent the afternoon dossing around or cleaning and washing my gear. A new guy has arrived, another Brit called Gary. He seems a bit quiet, and not the type to be here, time will tell. He was initiated by Dave and John who sent him down the well, to retrieve the bucket after the rope snapped, then made him fill the shower tank with around fifty buckets of water, that should keep him amused for a while. In the evening Pepi-Joe came around to cook a pig on our spit, it must be Sunday! After waiting four hours for it to cook it was soon demolished, or at least the half Radek had left us while picking at it; 'Radek like food!' Whilst there Pepi-Joe let Tom know that he had passed a message onto his wife and let her know he was OK. Apparently he used a car phone, being used in Bijela and got through to the UK. Tom has now stolen our truck and is heading towards Bijela. The beer began to flow, but I managed only three before disappearing to my bed as Ron and I have volunteered for a recce patrol tomorrow assisting the Bijela team. I got up early next morning, Radek was already up, and Ron soon joined us. Then Boby popped in to tell us the recce patrol was off, he left hurriedly followed by verbal abuse from Ron, not a happy Canadian! The others had stayed up until after 1:00am on the Rakia, it had also rained heavily during the night. So we got stuck into the clear up operation after last night's party. It looks like an artillery shell has exploded in the garden: with chairs, tables, crockery and food everywhere. Those responsible are still in bed and won't rise until midday. Nikolas had appeared at our place sometime during the night, and sat around during the clean up. I don't know the French for give us a hand you idle frog twat!

Our new guy Gary has not created a good first impression of himself, apparently last night, according to the sore heads when they got up. He had told them he had gone AWOL from the British army after a year, and joined the Legion, but was soon caught out on that story. I said that his year in the Brits must be true though, because he had told me earlier that he had been a storeman in the Royal Army Ordnance Corps, and nobody in their right mind would brag about being in that lot! Anyway his time here has been terminated and he is being sent to the Bijela team as a volunteer cook.

At 4:55pm a major panic started. Boby came around in his pick up truck and informed us of a shooting incident near to Donji Rahic. The four of us left, from our team, myself, Ron, Radek and Tom were on the truck five minutes later as Boby drove us on the twenty minute journey to the area. Dave and John were out in our truck somewhere on a beer buying mission. We arrived at Donji Rahic to find that a Chetnik patrol had hit three civilians making Rakia at a still just forward of our line, the three men all in their fifties had gone to check on their still they had secretly been using, unfortunately they had been seen or heard. On our arrival we found one had been shot dead, one wounded, shot through both legs, and one poor sod missing, probably taken by the Chetniks. There was nothing we could do, the wounded man was taken away for treatment, and we searched the area for signs of the missing man but found nothing. The dead mans body was taken away by the local guard. Another stupid loss. We returned an hour later and went straight to the cookhouse for our stew ration, and then back to our house.

At 9:15pm, Dave and John returned with Gaston and Nikolas, all of them a bit worse for wear. They had obviously found a watering hole and drank it. I went to bed early, because if the operation does go ahead we will have to be up early. The idea is to dominate the village of Gorice and the surrounding area in force, using all available local troops. While some civilians go in and retrieve a large supply of dried pig and animal feed.

Sounds exciting! Ron fell out with Dave over the booze situation and told him that after the operation tomorrow, he is going to Bijela to work with them for a few days.

16.

I woke everybody up at 3:45am, leaving at 5:00am after our caffeine injection. We travelled by vehicle this time to a position 500 metres south of Gorice. Tadia, one of the Croatians who travelled with us from Zagreb was at this position, we said our hello's before moving off in single file on foot to Gorice. As we entered the village we crossed a bridge covered with anti-tank mines, though we only found out about these later when we saw them in daylight. When it was dark we trampled all over them, luckily a man can't detonate an anti-tank mine, he's not heavy enough, but it still would have been nice to have known they were there.

As we moved into the centre of the village, Dave told me to take Radek plus four Croatians and set up an ambush position on the single track road coming into the village from the north, as this was the most likely route to be used by the Chetniks.

Once my group was in position I gave them arcs of fire and told them not to shoot until I gave the order. We then settled in to wait. Half an hour later we could only watch, amused, as Gaston, Pepi-Joe and two Croatians moved through our killing area, obviously not knowing our position and without any idea of what was happening. They settled into waiting positions 200m further up the road. As Gaston's group were in our arcs of fire I could do nothing other than back them up if needed and quickly lost interest, so I went for a root in a wrecked and looted house near my position, in which I found a complete chess set, a pack of cards and a rare tin of boot polish. Radek, just as bored as I was, and probably even more in the dark than me, was looking very depressed so I challenged him to a game of chess which I promptly lost. After about two and a half hours in position we were told to withdraw. The pig food had been wheel-barrowed across the bridge (around the mines) to a waiting tractor and trailer and ferried off. The mission was now complete. On our way back, two of the Croats with us caught a goat each and we threw them on the back of the truck. Later in the afternoon after a kip, one of the captured goats, the pretty little white one with blue eyes, was killed, cooked and eaten. It was he first time I have eaten goat and I'm looking forward to the next time. Ron has spoken to me again about working in

Bijela for a few days, we can't go until tomorrow, and then we'll have to hitch a lift but we both agree it'll be better than staying here.

I finally beat Radek at chess this evening and then lost to Tom. Stupid game anyway! No alcohol for the troops tonight, as none to be found. I was up early again the next morning to catch the English news, Britain may be sending a UN force to Bosnia. I don't know what I think about that yet, it's hard to see what they could do. I know there's a field ambulance unit here already, but that's in Zagreb, Croatia. Ron is already up and none too happy. He fell out with Dave again last night because Dave told him he couldn't go to Bijela. He said that there may be a Chetnik offensive in the next twenty-four hours so we are needed here – Rons reply was simply... 'BULLSHIT!' Gaston and Nikolas have gone back to Bijela, we should have gone with them, but we have decided to stay and see what happens about this apparent 'new offensive' and then leave early tomorrow.

We heard today that there is fighting North of Krepsic in the town of Vidovice. It is believed the town is about to fall to our HV forces, the noose is maybe tightening on the Chetniks here, are we in with a chance of winning? Andreas woke me at 5:30am, along with Drago (the local commander of Bijela). We were told to throw our kit on and be ready in five minutes. Dave was woken early like the rest of us, and thinking this was an authorized deployment, told Drago he could take myself, Radek, Tom and Ron. He would remain here with John in this area and provide mortar back-up if required. The mortar was now in permanent readiness, stored on our truck with twenty-five bombs. I grabbed my kit, the AK-47 and sniper rifle, jumped into Drago's minibus and set off. Tom has brought the OSSA and Radek is carrying two spare rockets. We were told we were heading for an area called Podbari, just west of Polijaci, arriving an hour later at Podbari we went into a small church that was being used as a base for the local guard there. Once inside we met up with the rest of the Bijela team, Joe, Lars, Broadmoor, Gary and Nikolas. Gaston was at Dubrava with the BST cannon and local troops.

We were quickly briefed on today's operation. Later in the morning, Bosnian troops from Tuzla would start the attack on Cerik from the southern end. Our job was to penetrate the enemy held area and hit the main road on the northern side of Cerik, the road that runs between Cerik and the Chetnik stronghold of Pelagicevo. We were to carry out our attack before the Bosnian troops went in, in the hope of drawing out troops from Cerik and Pelagicevo. We were then to hold our position for 30 minutes. The Bosnian troops would then mount their assault from the south. The plan sounded good except for the fact that we may have to hold at least 150 enemy soldiers, odds of 15-1, not bad odds… for them!

We moved out in single file across country and through no man's land until we came to a small hamlet of twelve houses. We checked the area with binoculars before moving any closer. This was actually the village of Podbari, it seemed deserted. The local inhabitants had fled long ago, and we could see no sign of enemy movement. We moved slowly into the village and began a check of the houses. The village was indeed deserted. We moved through it and into the fields on the other side, all over the fields were markers which had skulls and crossbones with the word 'MINEN' painted underneath though no mines were seen. We crossed the fields using the hedgerows which also gave us a small amount of cover, then moved into and through a wood until we came to the tree line on the far side. We positioned ourselves along the tree line, thankfully the local scouts had brought us to a good position overlooking the main road which could clearly be seen about 250 metres across the open ground in front of us. There was also three half built houses about a hundred metres away to our right, the centre one had a Serbian flag mounted on the chimney stack. This house must be manned although we couldn't see any movement, though as it was only 7:30am so they may still be in their beds.

We had now spread out along the tree line. I was on the left of the line, with only Broadmoor and one of the local scouts I had not seen before to the left of me. To my right were Tom and Radek, who had found a small ditch and a thick tree stump for cover where they were to use the OSSA, on the right of them were Joe and Lars with the RPG 7 (complete with new firing pin). Then came Andreas, Gary, Ron, Nikolas and Pelec, the second Croatian, but where Drago had got to, I didn't know. The attack started as soon as the first vehicle, a light truck, came down the road towards Cerik, Tom kicked it off by firing the OSSA. The rocket exploded on the road, peppering it with shrapnel. Simultaneously we all opened fire, the vehicle span off the road, into a ditch. We then focused our attention on the houses. Two machine gun emplacements on the road, one about 300m away to the left and the other about 500 metres away to the right, began to return fire into our tree line. The heavy calibre 7.9mm bullets tore into the trees above us, causing us to keep our heads down, the soldiers in the houses to our front, then began to return fire. There was, at least, one light machine gun, several AK-47s and at least one sniper returning fire. The noise was becoming deafening; our rifles hammering away, incoming rounds cracking around us and ricocheting off trees or smashing into them. Tom fired another OSSA rocket toward the nearest machine gun on the road but it failed to explode. Lars put an RPG 7 rocket through a window of the left hand house. I was busy swapping rifles, sometimes firing bursts of automatic from my AK at the two machine guns or putting single rounds through the doors and windows of the houses with the sniper rifle. This was becoming one hell of a fire fight, and we were giving as good as we got. After about ten minutes some of the occupants of the houses decided to scram, two cars set off from the front of the buildings in great haste, they were out of our sight but could clearly be heard driving away rapidly. Maybe they had taken casualties or maybe they were just scared, we didn't know. The battle lulled, with only occasional bursts of fire from the centre house. There were maybe four or five still in there, and somewhere in one of the houses was a sniper with big balls, and he was a good shot. He seemed intent on getting Tom or Radek, putting rounds into the tree stump they were behind. I searched for him through my sniper scope and began putting rounds through windows or small cracks in the roof tiles, trying to find him. He found me and shot off a branch six inches above my head, this certainly got my attention and I rolled away from the tree I was using for cover and moved behind another even deeper into the woods and continued trying to find him. I never did find out where he was firing from and he has my respect for that, the bastard. The lads could hear my little battle with the sniper because the boom from the .308 rifle was a heavier noise than the AK's. Ron shouted 'get the fucker, Steve' but I just couldn't find him, nobody could. He was good. From the road came the sound of heavy lorries and armoured vehicles bringing reinforcements. We could hear orders being shouted as troops debussed the vehicles, from the sound of this lot, now deploying on the far left of our wood, the plan to draw troops out of Cerik was working. We were still busy engaging the houses and two machine guns plus any vehicles, speeding along the road. On one occasion a transporter armoured personnel vehicle showed itself before Lars sent it back into cover after narrowly missing it with an RPG 7 rocket. Drago had reappeared, and fearing an infantry assault from the left ordered myself, Nikolas, Broadmoor, Andreas and Lars 50 metres deeper into the left hand side of the wood, to face the expected assault.

We scrambled into our positions just as the Praga came into play. The 30mm and 50 mm cannon tearing into the trees, the exploding shells impacting and scything them in half. It was an awesome sight, the top halves of the trees falling left and right into each other. Then mortar shells started impacting in the wood, some of the mortar bombs were airburst shells, detonating about twenty feet up, sending branches flying in all directions. Tom said from his position, that it was a sight to see, the flashes and bangs above our position and then trees falling left and right. This was getting out of hand, the tide had turned and now we were on the receiving end of the fire fight. The noise now was absolutely deafening, with the Praga firing, mortar and airburst shells detonating, trees and branches cracking and breaking, automatic fire coming from the road and houses, plus the additional automatic fire now coming in from the left and the now debussed troops. Bullets and shrapnel flew in all directions as we were resigned to lying face down, gripping the ground behind whatever cover we had found. I was just waiting for the pain or shock as a round or splinter of shrapnel hit me. Then strangely, there was another lull in the battle so Drago ordered us out of the woods. Rifle and AK47 fire was still coming in but it had dwindled, the mortars and Praga fire had stopped. As I got up to move I looked around me, the tree I was behind had taken a direct hit from a 30mm Praga shell although I had not heard it, the noise being so intense. The top half of the tree was leaning into another tree and had luckily for me, not slipped and pinned me to the ground. I could see Broadmoor, Drago, Andreas and Lars. I asked Drago where the rest of the team were, and he said he had told them to go earlier, as they were carrying the heavier equipment. I knew that at least one person had got away safely earlier, the Croatian who had been on the left of myself and Broadmoor had fled at the start of the initial fire fight leaving only a patch in the grass where he had lain until the shooting started. We withdrew slowly from the woods, ducking and diving as rounds came in from both directions. We left the wood and moved quickly across the first field towards our lines. I couldn't see the rest of the team, when we got to the hedgerow I looked across the second field and still could not see them, I could feel something was wrong so I ran to the front of our spaced out line and stopped Drago. I told him that the others could not have crossed this ground so quickly carrying the anti-tank weapons. He assured me they were in front of us, but I could see I was looking into frightened eyes and I didn't believe him. I went back to the hedgerow with Broadmoor and Lars and shouted twice to Tom and Radek. I received no reply. The second time I shouted we received more incoming rifle fire from the Chetniks who by now could have entered the woods themselves. Drago was nearing the houses at Podbari, but this was still 1000 metres from the safety of our lines. The three of us ran up to him and demanded that we stop at the first house, until we found the others. We waited by the house for five minutes before myself, Lars and Andreas decided to return to the woods to look for them. As we made our way across the nearest field we saw them coming towards us, it was a relief to see they were all there and in one piece to say the least, although burdened with the heavy equipment. We later found out that Drago had ordered us out but had not informed them, even though he said he had called out to them to go. They themselves had lost sight of us when we had moved away to the left of them as we faced the expected infantry assault. Tom, Radek, Ron, Joe, Nikolas and Pelec, then realised they had been deserted and had gamely collected the equipment between them, before carrying it out under fire. Drago had not only left them, but lied to us by saying they had already bugged out. Now as a complete unit we headed for the safety of our lines, Drago led the way.

On our arrival there we were treated to our first coffee of the day and half an hour later breakfast arrived. With all the running about I had done, and as it got hotter, I could not face stew. I went into the cool church basement to try to sleep. Later Drago came in to try and give us a pep talk. We had cut the road for over an hour and they still were not using it, we also succeeded in drawing out 16 trucks or armoured vehicles from Cerik, all laden with troops. The attack on Cerik from the south had now supposedly begun although I didn't hear much noise coming from that direction. Drago had now miraculously recovered his hero stance, though I would never forget the fear and panic in his eyes. Later in the morning, possibly just to get us out of the way, Drago decided to send us forward again to Podbari to keep a look out for any Chetnik vehicle movement or patrols. We knew the area near Podbari could not have any vehicles in it, because the bridge on the track into Podbari from the main road was down, blown by the Serbs long ago, though we went anyway just to amuse him! Before setting off Andreas produced a spent 7.62mm round from the inside of his boot, the round was probably one of this mornings ricochets, had gone through the leather but not pierced the skin. Another lucky escape for Andreas, who has already been wounded twice in the same leg from an anti-personnel mine, escaping with minor injuries on that occasion. We re-entered the small village after confirming it was still deserted. I began looking for a good sniper/lookout position in case any enemy foot patrols may be prowling the area, and broke into the small school building to look for a good vantage point but could not find a suitable position. I was just about to leave when Tom, who had followed me in decided to answer the call of nature. He had just dropped his trousers and had assumed the crouch position, when he fell through the floorboards. I tried and really tried not to laugh too much because I don't think he immediately saw the funny side!

I eventually found a good position in an upstairs room of a house opposite the school (downwind of Tom)! Ron and Radek had now joined me; they were wearing their looting heads, and had found two tins of fruit cocktail which we soon demolished. I joined in the search for spare rations and after rummaging through the previous owners belongings we all had our booty of coffee, sugar, soap, shampoo and some miniature bottles of spirits, which the owner had obviously enjoyed collecting, then settled down to wait.

Drago appeared later once he had decided it was safe, and thought it would be a good idea to go back to the woods to check if the Chetniks were using the road again, and if so repeat the action. We were none too happy about going back to a previously used position., but after a quick discussion, we agreed to go only for a look, and set off once more for the now depleted tree line, facing the main road. We left our newly acquired goods behind, to be collected on our return. Thankfully whilst back in our own lines earlier we had taken the time to fully replenish our ammunition. Drago had, of course, chosen himself to stay behind with Broadmoor to guard this village position. Pelec the only remaining Croatian came with us. The guy that had fled earlier, who we now nicknamed 'grass patch', had refused to come out with us again. I can understand some of these guys being wary of us; they don't know us and probably think we are all crazy! That is why we always found it better to work with the Croats who we knew from our adopted villages. We moved cautiously across the fields, through the wood and up to the tree line once more. We took up our positions again and stayed there for over an hour, unseen, we hoped. The three houses now seemed deserted. The only traffic using the road during that time were four civilian cars travelling very fast out of Cerik. Some intermittent gunfire, could be heard from the south of Cerik, but it did not sound as though any major offensive was being fought for the town. We decided to move back. Me being my usual doom and gloom self, expecting to be ambushed all along the route back to the houses at Podbari.

17.

Back in relative safety we settled down in the shade for a break. Someone decided to tell our brave commander Drago, that on the second visit we could have taken the three houses. He left with the idea of getting some troops to help with this new task. I suspect that one of the Bijela team put the idea into his head, although nobody would dare admit to it. No one was happy with this plan as it meant returning to our original positions for a third time, then having to cross 100 metres of open ground which was covered by the two machine guns on the road, then after taking the houses which may still be manned, we would set them alight and retreat back into the wood, crossing the open ground again, which by this time would be under Praga fire. All this to just to set fire to some houses, it seemed pointless and even suicidal to me.

Drago eventually re-appeared with twenty-one Bosnian troops from somewhere, telling us all to tie light blue armbands round our right arms for identification purposes. We then sat down to listen to Drago's plan translated to us by Andreas. In this plan he had somehow not got himself involved, Joe stating; ' he has got a yellow streak down his back wide enough to take a T-84 tank'. I was selfishly happy, that I was not to be part of the assault-come-suicide group. Although I had another task. The plan involved three teams. One consisting of the Bosnians minus one, a man called Brada, a local guy, who would be with me. This twenty man team along with Nikolas would assault the houses, covered by the support team of Ron, Tom, Radek, Lars and Broadmoor in the tree line. The support team would then hit the left hand machine gun bunker, and then move past the hopefully captured houses and onto the road. They would then fire down the road at any reinforcements. Myself and Brada would get into a position where we could hit the right hand machine gun 600 metres away. I was to use a Russian LAW the new version of the 64mm LAW, as yet untried by us, but it should be ideal for the job.

We set off all together across the fields until we reached the edge of the wood, where Brada and I left the other two teams. Brada led the way through fields and small woods until I found he had brought me to within 150metres on the far side of the machine gun position, which was in a house on the other side of the road to us, and well within range of the light anti-tank weapon (LAW). We found a good firing point with decent cover alongside some empty pig pens at the side of the road.

The only problem I foresaw was if the gun position was on the left hand side of the house, we were to the right of the house therefore the rocket may penetrate one wall but not two if the house had a dividing wall upstairs. We sat back and waited for the attack by the other teams to begin; I took off the end covers of the launcher and sat back. When we heard the other teams open fire some 600 metres away Brada moved up alongside the pig pens, his AK47 at the ready. As soon as I fired the rocket he would open up on the gun position with automatic fire. I gripped the launcher with both hands and pulled it apart to extend and arm it. I put the launcher onto my shoulder, sighted onto the upper wall on the side of the house and pressed the trigger... WHOOSH! The rocket flew toward the building and detonated in a cloud of black smoke on the wall! Brada began firing at the front balcony with his AK47, I threw the launcher aside and quickly picked up my AK47, set the safety to automatic and fired one long burst of thirty rounds toward the position as had Brada. I ducked back down behind the pig pens to change my magazine and stayed there as two bursts of fire were returned in our direction. Not exactly at us, as we had not been seen, but the smoke hanging in the air from the rocket backblast gave us away slightly. The rocket had woken them up, but not done them any damage; I could see a foot wide hole in the blackened upper wall. The machine gunner stopped firing after the two short bursts, so we both emptied another magazine toward the position in bursts of 8-10 rounds. This time strangely, we received no return fire. We again changed magazines and focused on the building, suddenly only seconds later, three men ran from the back of the house, one carrying an RPK machine gun and two with AK47's. The three, all Chetnik militia men, from the mixture of their uniforms, were all bunched together, darting through the cover of bushes behind the house, and had got about 70 metres from the rear of the building, running diagonally across our front. We both fired simultaneously into the three as they came into view, only 80 metres away. All three went down immediately. I heard at least one piercing scream of terror and pain. They disappeared from our view into the knee high undergrowth and the dust kicked up by our rounds hitting the ground around them, I don't believe they could have known, we were this close to them, they probably thought the rocket had been fired from further away. I fired another burst of five rounds into the area they had fallen, Brada emptied his magazine. We could not see any movement, but nor could we see any bodies, Brada looked at me and ran his fingers across his throat. I shrugged and said 'maybe', just as one of them stood and made a dash for freedom. I raised my AK quickly, and fired another well aimed burst of 6-7 rounds until the magazine clicked empty, at the fleeing figure. I knew I had hit him at least once; the sound of an impacting high velocity 7.62mm round hitting solid flesh is not a nice one! He let out a scream and pitched forward into the undergrowth, as I quickly changed magazines again. We kept a watch on the area, and for about a minute we could hear a low pitched, frightened moaning, someone was hurt, and then silence. After another minute I decided to lob a grenade into the area, to flush anyone out, as we could not cross the road to check on them, because if the other teams attack had gone as planned. The support team may already be on the road prepared to fire at anything that moved on it. I took a grenade from one of the holders on my jacket, pulled the pin and lobbed it into the area they had fallen. Just as I was beginning to think I had thrown a dud, and after what seemed an eternity, but probably just seconds, the grenade exploded with a crump. It had fallen 5 metres short of where the militia men had fallen; grenades are not as easy to throw accurately over a distance. Still nothing moved. I didn't feel good at what had just happened, and Brada did not have the look of the conquering hero either, this was shit! I had only one more spare magazine left, I would have to watch my ammunition from now on, one on my AK, one spare - 60 rounds left, I had used 90 rounds already, I flicked my safety onto single shot, and signalled to Brada to do the same, it was only then, that he realised he still had an empty magazine on his weapon. The recent events had stunned us both. We watched and waited, I was not happy. The attack on the houses seemed to have stopped. If it had gone as planned there should have been more shooting. Unless, of course, they had met the same feeble resistance we had, the machine gun crew we hit must have thought they were going to be overrun by a larger force, or else they may have thought we had two rockets, and about to try again. I didn't know at the time that Nikolas and Andreas had stopped the attack for fear of heavy casualties. The three houses had been reinforced, including our friend the sniper who nearly ended it all for Radek. The Bosnians though, were all ready to go in, brave but foolish! After waiting a while longer, Brada started laughing and pointed behind me, my bush hat was lying about ten metres away in tatters, I had stupidly put in on the floor as I put in my ear defenders to fire the launcher. I had left my hat in the backblast area when I had moved forward into my firing position, normally I would have left it, but my cap badge from my old regiment was on it, another one of my lucky talismans. I ran back and picked up the tatters but my badge was nowhere in sight, I guess somebody will find it one day and wonder what the Queen's Lancashire Regiment was doing here! I stuffed the tattered remains of my hat in my pocket and went back to my position, hopefully unseen. We waited in this position for a further twenty minutes, and I was continually on edge, waiting for troops to turn up to find out what had happened to their comrades. Had we killed them all? Were there wounded? Had they crawled away? Or worse still, one or more still out there, unseen by us? I could easily frighten myself to death sitting here with someone I can't even speak to. We have to rely on sign language to communicate.

Eventually we set off back to Podbari cautiously, probably both wondering the same thing: are we going to walk into an ambush? I heard firing up ahead from a rifle on single shot, Brada leading the way moved into cover. The shots were tapped out in a familiar tune. It was Tom's favourite shooting tune and I realised that it was a signal for us to come in. I walked up to Brada, now down on one knee, and told him it was OK, at which he moved forward again, a minute later Tom played his tune again. He looked to me for reassurance, I nodded and we plodded on again. When Tom finally fired a third signal Brada had learnt it and we carried on into Podbari. It was here we found out about the attack being stopped, we then set off together for our lines. Tom told me that Radek had been very upset at pulling back. He kept asking, 'Why we go Tom? Why no shoot Chetniks?' He had also been very lucky. He stood up to fit his rocket carrier onto his back when the sniper put one into the tree only inches from his face. Radek isn't stupid and he certainly doesn't lack courage. He is young, eager and lacks only experience, his reply to the Chetnik sniper was, to shout 'Fuck off, Chetnik bastard!' Back at the church buildings Drago put our Donji Vuksic team in his minibus and drove us back. He thanked us on the way and told us that the main Bosnian forces had taken and now controlled the area, to the south of Cerik.

Back at our house we were unloading our gear when Boby turned up. He didn't look too happy and he started arguing with Drago. Not understanding the lingo I just got my gear and took it to my room then went for a coffee which John had started to make, it turned out that during the argument, Boby punched Drago which put him on his arse! The argument was because

Drago had come round this morning and led us to believe we were going on an authorised deployment. It wasn't. Boby later also explained that Drago would risk us going into any situation as long as he got the credit for it, not caring about our team's safety, though I think we'd already worked that out for ourselves. Good news of the day was that Gaston had hit and destroyed a T54/55 tank just outside Dubrava on the Cerik road. I went to bed thoroughly knackered.

I got up later than usual the next morning after a good night's sleep. I went outside, made a brew and sat around discussing yesterday's events with the lads. I proudly showed off the remains of my hat destroyed in the backblast of the launcher. As we talked a vehicle turned up, Joe and Jelenic got out. Here comes trouble, I thought. They had come to find out if they could use four of our team to help in taking the houses in the southern end of Cerik, possibly clearing the whole of Cerik tomorrow, ensuring the town is completely clear of Chetniks. They went to speak to Boby and Dave. Boby OK'd the idea; he must trust Jelenic more than Drago, I'm not sure I do. Dave told John, Ron, Tom and Radek to kit up. He asked me to stay behind as I had another job. When the others had left, Boby asked if it would be possible to blow a road using the explosives recovered from the wood near Gorice. I told him not without detonators, to which he produced a box of ten electric detonators! 'OK', I foolishly said, 'no problem' - me and my big mouth! He left me to make an improvised pressure pad. He had been given a mission to destroy the road between Cerik and Pelagicevo to stop Cerik being reinforced; we were to blow it tonight! He and Dave then left with two Croatians for a daylight recce of the area.

I went into the kitchen of our house and found an old cereal size box and some silver cooking foil; I placed two ten inch squares of the foil inside the box then taped one piece on each of the inner sides. I then took out a detonator, each one had two wires, red and blue attached. I wired the detonator up to a 6 volt radio battery, then attached a wire and taped it to each piece of foil, and back to the detonator. The detonator was pre-positioned in a hole of a tree outside, where I was working. I pressed the two sides of the box together and bang! The detonator exploded, that was my pressure pad! I replaced the detonator after resetting the box and waited for Boby and Dave to return. Today is the expiry date of my train ticket home. I don't think I'll make the train today - somehow! Maybe next month, touch wood.

Boby and Dave got back three hours later and said they had found a good position to blow the road, where there was a large drainage pipe below the road. They said also the area either side of the road was soft marshy ground so once the road had been blown no vehicles could pass. I gave them a demonstration of my home made trigger, the pressure pad. Boby seemed impressed and set off to the HQ at Ulice to inform them it was on. When he returned he told us that we would leave at 3am. He, Dave and the two Croatians who had been on the recce would provide a cover group for me to go forward and place the device. Nice! I thought. I had dropped myself right in it. The team got back at 9:00pm. They had had a busy day. All four of them had been with the Bijela team, working as one unit, clearing houses on the southern end of Cerik and securing the area. Local Croatian forces and Bosnian troops from Tuzla had all taken part. The main town of Cerik was now our next target.

The Chetniks lost ten men today, one of them claimed by John who took him out with his sniper rifle. We only had one casualty; it was poor Brada who I had been with yesterday. He was wounded by shrapnel; although how bad he is we don't know yet. I hope he makes it.

The lads also returned with some freshly acquired goodies, three rifles, plenty of coffee and sugar. Of course the day my team had again dished it out, instead of taking it, was the day I had to stay behind. Not a good day for me after all. I got up at 2am to prepare for my 3 o'clock start. I packed the battery, my home-made pressure pad, the remaining eight detonators, and a garden trowel into my Bergen, and picked up the AK47 and my fully replenished magazines. One of Boby's lads was going to borrow my sniper rifle; luckily Dave and I were ready when Boby turned up half an hour early. We jumped into the back of his four wheel drive Toyota pick up truck where there were already four of the local Croats in the back and another up front with Boby driving. The box of explosives was also lying in the back of the truck, and as it bounced along the dirt tracks we took to the drop off point I knew I would be glad to dispose of it! Boby pulled up alongside an old farm building about six hundred metres from the target road. In this building were housed a six man Croatian guard unit. All were asleep on our arrival, Boby dropped off two of his guys here, to give us cover out to the road, one had my sniper rifle. I thought they would not be much good to us, being six hundred metres in front of them in the dark, but I kept my gob shut. Boby set off towards the road with Dave and myself behind him. Two unarmed Croats carrying the box of explosives and one carrying a PAP bolt action rifle, bringing up the rear, not much of a cover group I thought. Boby led us to the edge of a tree line 40 metres away from the road. As we lay in the tree line listening for enemy movement, I could feel the ground was damp and boggy; the 40 metres of open ground between us and the road looked to have puddles on it that glistened in the moonlight. Once the area was deemed to be clear I placed my AK47 on the top of the box of explosives, grabbed the rope handles at each end, and began my trip alone, out on the road side. Leaving the cover group of five men with three weapons behind me. As I stepped out in the night lugging the kit with me I realised very quickly I was crossing a muddy bog. The 'puddles' I had seen earlier was water that had risen to the top of the mud and settled. As I noisily made my way to the roadside the cold water and mud poured over and into my boots. I inwardly cursed at those behind me probably giggling away at my attempts to stay on my feet, it seemed my heart was pounding louder than the noise I was making with my feet as I got to the roadside. I could easily see the drainage pipe that Boby had earlier pointed out. I placed the box by the pipe entrance. I picked up my AK and knelt down to listen for any movement in six inches of cold wet slimy mud. 'Of course I can make a pressure pad Boby!' - You big gobbed prat I thought to myself. I waited two to three minutes listening quietly for any movement from either end of the road. I knew the other side of the road from my position was of the same muddy shit as the stuff I was knelt in now. No one else would be daft enough to be sat in it tonight, the only noises came from my own cover group behind me, someone coughed and I heard Boby say Shush!!' Louder than the cough! I love it here! I took off my Bergen and placed it next to the box of explosive. I put my AK down alongside it out of the mud, and began to push the explosives into the drainage pipe. I got about six feet into the pipe below the road then pulled the lid off and exposed the plastic explosive. The bottom of the drainage pipe was covered in a two inch thick wet slime, and as I crawled back I found it had run up my sleeves, and that the front of my clothes were coated in it, by now I was really wet and really pissed off. I cleared a patch of gravel from the top of the road, and pushed it into a pile, then leant over the roadside and began to chip away at the hard packed earth, to dig a hole for my pressure pad box, stopping every couple of minutes to listen to see if I had attracted any attention from either end of the road. It took over twenty minutes, as I was told later, to dig the hole deep and wide enough to take my 'pad'. It seemed much longer. Finally the hole was large enough to take my box. I pushed a two inch long twig between the inner sides of the box, to help take the weight of the gravel which I pushed over and around it. When I was satisfied that it was as well hidden from sight as I could tell, in the darkness, I covered the wires leading from it smearing them in the mud, then pushed them into the drainage pipe and onto the explosive box lid, that was just above the wet slime. I then packed my Bergen up, and made sure that I had left no tell tale signs of my visit, before crawling back into the drainage pipe, connecting the battery wires, then, with an outstretched arm pushed the detonator into the explosive, and crawled quickly out. I made sure the box lid, battery and any excess wire were inside the pipe entrance and out of casual sight, then picked up my Bergen and AK47 and set off noisily back through the bog. I didn't want to hang around here too long, now that it's primed and ready to go. I got wetly back to my so called cover group, who were all surprisingly awake. Dave said to me casually; 'I thought you'd fucked off home.' Boby led the way back to the farm buildings, the trip back warmed me up a bit, but I was still soaking wet. It was 5:30am when we arrived back at the farm buildings, and the guard was just rising from their slumber. Boby's two lads were still awake though, and he told them to keep watch on the road, and report immediately to him on the radio, if there was any success.

We then piled into his truck and set off back, for the twenty minute drive to Donji Vuksic. Back at our village Boby got a brew on, but I declined the offer, and walked back to our house to change out of my mud sodden clothing. Dawn was breaking, as I risked a bitterly cold shower and changed into dry clothes. I was just about to walk down to Boby's at 7:46am, when I heard the detonation. John came out of his room opposite mine and said 'What was that?' I smiled and said 'I've been playing!' As I walked down to Boby's I hoped I had not hit any civilian vehicles, not that any should be around. I wanted to have hit, a nice ammunition truck, tank, praga vehicle or an armed Chetnik patrol. Boby came running up the road, clutching his Motorola radio, to greet me. Grinning widely, he said 'Steve you kill a big Chetnik.' 'It worked then', I said, still laughing he said, 'You kill a PIG! Ha Ha!' Apparently three stray pigs had wandered down the road, the last one, triggered the explosion. The good news was that first reports are good, and the road is impassable to wheeled vehicles. Boby is going to check later, when he collects his two lads, from the guard position. At 9:00am while we sat outside making coffee and the lads were telling their stories from yesterday, Jelenic turned up and asked for four volunteers. A tank was known to be still in the area around Cerik. the tank may be stranded because the road was blocked after the road was blown earlier. There are also a few more houses to be cleared on the southern outskirts of Cerik.

Not wanting to be left behind again, I went straight to my room and started to kit up. Tom got the babysitting job and was told to stay behind with Dave. John, Ron, Radek and I got aboard the minibus with Jelenic. He had commandeered the minibus from the now mysteriously absent Drago. We set off for Cerik via Bijela, arriving on the southern outskirts of Cerik at 10:00am. We were led up to a building which had been taken over for use as their HQ. We waited outside, hoping to be told what was happening, half an hour later, the Bijela team arrived to join us. Only Gaston, Joe, Lars, Andreas and Broadmoor turned up. I asked where Nikolas and Gary were. Joe said that Nikolas was working with Francois' group from Jagodnjak who were somewhere around here. Gary had been left behind in Bijela, apparently he had flipped his lid yesterday, crying at the sight of the dead bodies, they had given him a day off to sort himself out. Unfortunately it looks like yesterday was Gary's first and last action. We were told later that Nikolas had been shot and wounded while working with Francois' group earlier in the morning.

18.

Just after 11:00am we were told to form up and move into Cerik, along with a Croatian section of ten men. We were told to move up through the static line of Croatians to the far end of the town where two Croatian soldiers had been killed during the night.

As we moved up the road and deeper into Cerik, rounds were cracking past and above us, I was hoping that these were just stray rounds. I remember wondering where they were coming from, as we were still well behind our forward positions, or so we had been told. We moved closer, trying to ignore this rifle fire, the cracks now getting closer, the Croatians led us off the road and across some fields until we turned right. We were now moving along the western side of the town, using hedgerows and dead ground to stay out of sight then we turned right again, advancing on to the west of the town. We then formed up into an extended line, with the Croatian section on our right, and swept up towards the buildings. As we moved up to the houses and into the outskirts of the town I saw three men standing at the side of a house, ahead of us. They were around 80 metres away, and stood watching us, as we moved up towards them, still in an extended line of which I was the right hand man. I looked across to the right, past our line, to the Croatian section, which had either dropped back or were lagging about twenty yards behind us. Our team was busy concentrating on the three Croatians or Bosnians ahead of us. These men were most likely the guard we had been told about earlier. As we approached them, moving past a deserted house and some pig pens, I had to move out further to the right to avoid us bunching up. I lost sight of the three men, but the centre of the line still had them in sight. The 'feeling' was wrong. I can't explain it, but later we all agreed; the 'vibes' were just wrong. The atmosphere had changed.

John, further down our line, was the nearest to them, now about 40m away. He called out to them, 'English – Ustasha', one of the three put his arm up and waved; but another one swung his AK up and at us, firing directly at our advancing line. At first they must have thought we, were other Chetnik troops coming in from another position to our left, which they, unbeknownst to us, had been setting up as an ambush position. Apparently we later learned that we had bumped into the 'Tigers' Chetnik Special Forces unit we had heard about a couple of weeks earlier.

As John called out to the men, we were all in open ground. When the shooting started I was forced to hit the deck in the

227

open ground and lay in six inches of grass wondering what was going on. Ron had managed to get back to the deserted house and pig pens we had just passed, and I knew Broadmoor and Lars were about ten yards behind me, as I had dashed forward before going to ground. I couldn't see the rest of the team because we had been well spaced out; Ron was at the side of the house looking forwards like me. I then saw one of the three Serbs bugging out to the left, I fired two or three rounds in his direction and shouted -'they're bugging out left.' I caught sight of Andreas who had found a ditch with Radek, Andreas threw two grenades towards the house in front of him. Suddenly machine gun fire started on our exposed left flank, the fire becoming very heavy. I stuck my face in the floor, hoping the ground would somehow open up and let me in, I could hear and feel rounds cracking past and around me, some of them zipping into the grass, kicking up tufts of soil. Somebody definitely had me in their sights, for once I didn't know what to do. I dare not move, and stayed very still, hoping that whoever was trying to kill me would think I had been hit. I was pinned down in a very exposed position and in metaphorical deep shit. I suddenly felt scared and vulnerable! After two or three minutes there was a lull in the fighting, Ron called across to me to see if I was OK. I told him I was, only to have to bury my face back in the dirt as more rounds came at me. They knew I was still there. Ron shouted at me to take my sniper rifle off my back because the barrel was sticking out above the grass, providing a good aiming marker, I struggled to get it off though, trying not to move and to stay as low as possible. I heard one of our team fire a 64mm LAW (Radek I found out later). It was a terrifying situation to be in, I felt totally exposed and a thousand thoughts went through my mind. I wished I could dissolve into the earth as I wondered when the first round would hit me. I couldn't move and I couldn't stay here, and didn't want to move, but knew I had to. I pushed the sniper rifle forward and over my head. As I did, two rounds slammed into the ground in front of me as I put the rifle down. Our team was now returning fire; Jelenic and Pelec had also come forward to Ron's position at the house. Jelenic shouted across to me and also to Broadmoor and Lars who were also pinned down and exposed, to crawl to our right and try to get into a cornfield about 30metres away. As I tried to move slowly to my right more rounds came at me, then I heard Andreas shout that they had taken a casualty. I decided to stay where I was, somebody had fired several smoke tromblones (rifle grenades), and smoke began to drift over us. I chose my moment to move, Joe and Gaston fired towards the enemy positions later found to be dugouts only 150m away. I got up onto one knee and fired one long burst from my AK to my left in the direction of the enemy fire, then picked up the sniper rifle and ran like hell toward the pig pens, closely followed by Lars and Broadmoor. I flung myself down and emptied my magazine. Ron, Pelec and Jelenic were now firing toward the enemy as Andreas brought out the casualty in a fireman's lift closely followed by Radek, I changed my magazine as Andreas arrived with Radek and the casualty. It was John.

John bringing up the rear of a patrol.

Now behind the pig pens near the house were myself, Andreas, John, Radek, Lars and Broadmoor. At the house were Ron, Jelenic and Pelec. Somewhere out front still, were Gaston and Joe. We stayed down behind the walls of the pig pens, which were only made of stone and clay and weren't safe enough to be behind, rounds were coming through them now and again. Still, it was a hell of a lot safer than where I had just been. Andreas, after very bravely carrying John to safety under fire, was gently putting him down, I saw that he had been hit at least twice. Ron, the section medic, ran across to help, Ron is a trained Legion medic. We checked the field dressings and tightened them, Radek and Andreas had applied them earlier before moving him. John had two wounds in his left leg, there was an entry and exit wound in his lower leg but a more severe wound higher up on his thigh, which was bleeding heavily. The bullet had exited at the base of his hip, Ron applied another dressing to this wound and then began to tie both his legs together, one to act as a makeshift splint for the other. I was busy talking crap to John, trying to reassure him, telling them that he would be OK, trying to stop him from going into shock. Jelenic and Lars had run across twenty metres of open ground under enemy fire and had come back with a door, on which to carry John until we found a stretcher. As I talked to John, he told me that the Chetnik who waved was wearing a HVO badge (Croatian Forces in Bosnia) and that they were in our type of camouflage uniforms. At that time we still did not know who had hit us. We were led to believe Croatian troops still held this area. After he had been patched up we placed John on the makeshift stretcher so that we could move him. All this time he never moaned or complained, he seemed to be taking it all very calmly. I thought of what it would be like if it were me on that door, would I be able to take it that well? I didn't want to know. Our next problem was to get him back. We were still under fire from our left although sporadically now. Jelenic called Joe and Gaston back to join us while we covered them. A plan was then formed to get John back, and out of further harms way. Jelenic, Radek, Ron and Lars would carry John across thirty metres of open ground to the cornfield. While Joe, Andreas, Broadmoor, Gaston, Pelec and myself would provide covering fire. From the cover of the cornfield, the stretcher team would get John back to the HQ buildings and medical aid. The section of Croatians had abandoned us long ago; I couldn't understand why or where they had gone. They should have and were told to move up on our right flank, the last I saw of them was prior to our contact with the enemy, just as they had started to lag behind. As the stretcher team positioned themselves for the dash across the cornfield, Andreas fired a smoke tromblone and they set off. We fired towards the enemy positions trying to cover the move as best as we could. I changed a magazine and saw that the stretcher party had made it across the open ground but Jelenic and Lars were busy trying to pull down a fence to get John through and into the cornfield. I continued to fire. Joe was stood at the corner of the pig pens, returning fire and I told him that he had better get down as the walls were not safe. Just as he did so, another 7.9mm machine gun round cracked through and covered his shoulder with dust. He told me later that he didn't bother saying anything to me at the time. We then heard shouting coming from the stretcher team, they had finally got into the cornfield and were now out of sight. The incoming fire now died down again and we waited in silence, listening for movement. I looked around me and on the floor, amongst the empty cartridge cases next to John's sniper rifle; I saw an empty but damaged AK magazine. I slung his rifle over my back along with mine; still cradling my AK-47 of which I now had only two full magazines left. I picked up the damaged magazine, it had been hit by a round, and it must have been full at the time because it had burst open. The bullet must have ricocheted away as there was no penetration of it. It must have been John's magazine. I put it in my pocket and thought about giving it to him later as a souvenir. Then we heard Jelenic shouting across to us, they were in trouble, Ron had been hit, and the door had broken in two, so they were now struggling with John. Jelenic was going back to get a stretcher and some help. Joe decided that we would have to pull back and help the stretcher team with the now two casualties, a good decision, as it was highly unlikely we would get reinforced and we were all low on ammunition. We moved back across to the cornfield one at a time, I was second to last; I got into the cornfield and covered the last man back, Gaston. We moved up to the stretcher team to find Radek and Lars struggling with John on a broken door. Ron was in cover, patching himself up. I asked him if he was OK, while the others went forward to find another door or something else on which to carry John. John was now in some pain but he was still silently taking it. Ron said he would be alright, he had also been shot through the leg but the bullet had not hit the bone, the entry and exit wounds were both clean. Once up on his feet, Ron was able to hobble by himself. A new door arrived; we got John onto it and carried him to some sheds and into better cover. I got some water from a well near the sheds and gave it to Ron and John, and poured the remainder over John's head while the wounded Ron, gave him a morphine shot. It had now been forty minutes since John had been hit, and I said we should move back ASAP. We struggled on with the stretcher, but it wasn't easy as John is a big lad, but all we could do was to keep changing round on the stretcher. The heat from the sun was beating down on us, and we were all exhausted but struggling slowly on. The sweat was pumping out of me as I was carrying one corner of the door, the AK in my other hand and two sniper rifles across my back, but we pushed on as fast as we could, still having to take cover every so often as we were still getting attention from the Chetniks. Pelec, the only Croat still with us, was keeping a rearguard and told us he had heard some Chetniks shouting close by. They were attempting to get round us and cut us off. We had to swing right, down and into a gully, then through a small wood. This was making the struggle even worse, the obstacles were getting bigger but finally, as we dragged John through the tree line and out onto a dirt track, six Croatians came running up with a stretcher. We put John onto the stretcher, and the Croats set off with John aboard. We followed on up the dirt track. The fields, either side of the track, were alight and burning, set off by what, I didn't know or really care. We shepherded Ron back, by now we were all thoroughly knackered. We had been in a bad spot, but we had got John out, after carrying him for a mile under fire and across country. Ron was now struggling a bit, as we had to dash over parts of the track that had caught fire. Radek took his webbing but, being the stubborn bastard that he is, Ron refused to give me his rifle until we finally got him to the makeshift ambulance at the HQ buildings.

We watched it leave with them both aboard, knowing that they now had a better chance, although it had now been an hour and a half since John had been hit. In all that time, he never moaned or complained, he just let us get on with the job of getting him back. What a bloke! Once they were away, we sat around to recover and relax a bit. I saw Pelec talking with some Croats. I walked up to him and thanked him for staying with us; I didn't even look at the other Croatians sat around. I walked back towards our team, just as Lars collapsed, unconscious, probably from heat stroke. We bundled him into a car and sent him off to the medical aid station some three kilometres away. Jelenic told us that with three men down and the rest of us physically exhausted, he would arrange transport back as soon as it was possible. He said we had done a good job and that now the

Bosnians were advancing into the Eastern side of Cerik once more. What good job had we done? I didn't know. We sat around talking, analyzing what had happened, trying to understand what we had done, what had gone wrong and why? All we really knew was that we were supposed to have been in controlled territory when we were hit. I had been carrying John's sniper rifle, as well as my own, on my back. When I took them off I noticed the damage to one of them. At first, I thought it was mine but it was John's rifle. It had been hit by a round. It had gone through the handgrip, behind the trigger, I then realised, from the way I knew he carried it, that he must also have taken a hit in the shoulder of his back. That made three wounds at least, plus the damaged magazine of his AK that I picked up earlier, he must have taken a right hammering. An hour later, Radek and I were on a borrowed minibus with John and Ron's kit. Heading back to Donji Vuksic, Radek told me exactly what had happened to John. He said that he didn't think he had been shot by one of the three that John had challenged at first, it was later, when they had managed to scramble forward into a ditch, along with Gaston, Joe and Andreas, and they began to return fire that John got up out of the ditch just as the Chetniks had fired from our left flank. John was hit by the initial machine gun burst, caught right in the middle of it, Radek said that the ground had erupted around him. Andreas and Radek had pulled him back into the ditch when he had gone down and gave him first aid; before they had brought him out whilst they themselves were under fire. On the way back to Donji Vuksic, we had to pass the medical station, so we stopped and went inside to see how the lads were doing. We found Lars, who was now recovering well, in fact he had a drip in one arm and a bottle of beer in his other hand and was sat up in bed. He was being tended to by a real woman, not often seen around here! He was doing fine. Worse news was that John and Ron had been sent on to the hospital at Gorni Rahic, another hour's drive across country. I began to worry about John's condition, as that road was in poor condition. Ron was OK, he would make it, but John had been hit three times at least and the time for treatment now had another hour added on. On arrival back at our house I told Tom what had happened, he had been completely unaware of our situation. He was concerned and asked his usual thousand questions but many of them could not be answered. Tom put a brew on for me and Radek and we sat for a while with our own thoughts. Dave and Boby had left earlier to check on this morning's damage that we caused to the road, I couldn't believe that that action was only this morning, it seemed like weeks ago now.

An hour and a half later, Dave came back from the HQ, with the news. John had died as the doctors worked on him, they had tried to revive him but could do nothing more, he had suffered serious internal bleeding from the wound in his thigh. The lower leg wound hadn't been too serious and his sniper rifle had deflected the shoulder wound which was not a major problem. It was the loss of blood and probably the shock. The treatment time didn't help; maybe he could have been saved if we'd had proper medical aid.

I believe the time we took to get him back was as fast as was possible under the circumstances, but once back at the HQ buildings or maybe even on the track back, there should have been medical treatment, not just a few first aiders. However, this is not an organised army with good logistical and medical back up, this is a civil war in a poor country, with doctors and medical supplies very scarce.

19.

After being told of John's death, I was stunned. I really wanted him to make it, and after we had got him to the ambulance, I thought he would. His condition was worse than we had first thought. It was his own strength that had kept him going for so long. It was only now that we were told about Nikolas. He had been moving into Cerik, before we had arrived, with Francois' group. Thinking the area was clear, as we had, he moved out from cover only to be shot twice. The first bullet should have killed him, he had been carrying his AK-47 across his chest in the ready to use position, and burst of fire came at him, one round hitting his Kalashnikov's breech block, which knocked him backwards. The second hit the wooden butt of his weapon, deflecting the bullet up into his forearm, passing through without hitting the bone. He was lucky, so was Ron, his leg wound was clean and we were told he would be back with us in three to four days.

Boby was excellent, without us knowing, he had been running round organising things that we hadn't even begun to think of. Later in the evening, he asked us where we would like to bury John, and it was decided that we would bury him near Boby's family plot at Lanista, one and a half kilometres from here. The burial would be tomorrow, and Boby would make further arrangements. Dave went off in the truck to inform the Bijela team. We sat around moping in our own thoughts, trying to piece the day's events together. What we have been told is that a group of 30-40 Chetniks including the 'special unit' had penetrated our guards defences the previous night in Cerik, and two Croats had been killed. Some of these men were wearing our type of camouflage uniforms; these were the men that we had walked into. The local forces gave up that ground during the night. The only good news we have heard, is that the strong Bosnian force attacked and retook Cerik from the east during the day. I have to think, knowing we came in from the west, that we may have been used to draw fire! Fifteen Chetnik bodies have been reported found in Cerik and many reported wounded after the Bosnian attack, the rest sneaking away. I hoped John's killer was among the dead! I honestly believe that during today's events, if the team that I was alongside today was a British Army section, then Andreas and Ronnie would most definitely have been decorated for their actions today.

I got up early the next day and cleaned and prepared my kit for John's funeral, to be held this morning. Before leaving for

Gorni Rahic, to collect John's body, we went round to the house where his coffin was being prepared. They sat us down and gave us coffee while the coffin was finished off. It had been made with good solid wood; from early this morning four of the local men had been making it in the best way they could, well before we were up. The five old women, still here in the village, had cleaned and prepared the interior with fresh sheets and blankets. All this was watched over by Boby. It seemed that no effort was being spared; they all wanted to do the best that they could. After the locals had finished off the coffin, we placed it on the back of Boby's pick up truck and with our team aboard we set off for Gorni Rahic. The Bijela team, who had heard the news, followed us down in their minibus. We went to the hospital to see if Ron was fit enough to come, of course he decided he was, though the doctor insisted that he returns this afternoon. I also found Brada, who was up and about and will make a full recovery, I'm glad about that after the incident a couple of days ago.

With Ron and crutches aboard, we went round to collect Johns body from the makeshift morgue. I didn't want to see him as I prefer to remember people the way they were, as did the other lads. It was left to Dave to collect the body and the relevant paperwork, while we waited outside, talking to Ron.

Before sealing the coffin, I put into it his knife and leather scabbard that had a sentimental meaning to him. I also put in a small Union Jack; John like myself, was very patriotic. We then draped the coffin with the Croatian flag, (none of us had a big enough Union Jack), then put it on the truck and set off back to Donji Vuksic. There wasn't much conversation on the route back. The service was held at the back of the command house, all the local people had turned out. It was a very respectful service and I was touched by the local people's sadness. After the service, we drove out to the church at Lanista; the burial was with full military honours. Our team formed the firing party.

We all said our goodbyes to John and he was laid to rest. Boby and Lars took some photos of the funeral and I have arranged for Dave to send them back when they are developed, for John's family who Dave is trying to contact. I don't know his family but I know they can be proud of him, and one day I hope to tell them so.

Johns Funeral Firing Party.

I only knew him for a few weeks but in that time I thought very highly of him and respected him. John was a big man in many ways.

When we returned from Lanista the locals had prepared food and drinks at our house. We thanked them for everything they had done for us today. John had a good send off and these people had made the effort. Later in the evening we went up to the north position for our usual Sunday pig roast. Although we were still down from the past two days events, we tried to make an effort but it wasn't the usual occasion. Worse still was that Gaston received a message from home that his eighteen month old daughter had drowned in an accident while he has been out here. It has not been a day to remember. Radek and I left early. Dave was getting drunk and wanted someone to blame for John's death, then again, don't we all? It's only the drink talking, who can you blame? This is a vicious war and people die. I can only hope there are no more deaths or injuries in our group, or among our own locals for that matter.

I woke up the next day with the idea of putting the past few days behind me. Today was to be a day off, but it didn't last long. I had just cleaned my weapons and had my combats in soak when I was asked if I could be ready in half an hour because I may be needed in Cerik. I had volunteered to go this evening if required. I decided not to be ready in half an hour and said no! I have learned a lesson just lately. No more quick kit on and then being thrown blindly into a situation in some town or village. I work here for the people of Donji Vuksic and its tactical area; we know we can trust the people here. In other places we have been used in emergencies, not just for our experience but because they don't want to risk their own. They don't feel a great allegiance to us as our own locals do, on occasions they have simply disappeared and left us to it in times of trouble. I may still go to Cerik this evening with Radek and a team from this village if I am needed. Dave and Tom are now going with Boby on a recce of the area and to position his local team. The line has been pushed forward and strengthened north of Cerik. Our people are needed as a forward line guard, while defence positions in and around Cerik are fortified. At 5:30pm Dave and Tom returned in the truck, they had a lucky escape while driving near Cerik. A mortar round exploded only yards ahead of the moving vehicle, fortunately nobody was hurt. Radek and I were asked to stay with the local Vuksic troops at Cerik overnight. We arrived there forty minutes later. The road our team is holding 2km north of Cerik is the main road we had been hitting from our positions in Dubrava, this was now our forward line with the Chetniks in new positions 400m further up the road. It seemed funny looking up at the positions we used to fire from, in and around the houses 500m away. The damaged T54/55 tank that Gaston hit a few days earlier is still here providing us with an excellent road block.

As Radek and I moved up to our forward positions, mortars were being fired onto those still in the Dubrava positions. The Bijela team was somewhere up there, like us, awaiting a possible counter attack. The mortars were being assisted by a tank which was out of sight just up the road. We sat in the dugouts that had once protected the Chetniks from our fire, as heavy fire was being directed down our road. We kept our heads down as it passed above us, and I ordered our locals through Mico, who speaks English, not to fire as there were no targets that could be seen to fire at. Ten minutes later, the firing became more intense, and I realised from my dugout position that we were taking incoming rounds from the woods running along the left hand side of the road. I told Mico to tell our locals to keep an eye out on our left flank but he said that he did not think anybody could have got to the left of us. After another two minutes of this Radek and I both thought 'bullshit', and stuck our AK's at arm's length over the side of the dugout and fired on automatic, Vietnam style, into the tree line. It seemed to work, as seconds later the firing stopped. I think they had tried to probe the line with fire to see if the defenders would pull back, but it didn't work! At around 9:00pm our team was relieved for the night by a Bosnian team from Tuzla. A right rag-tag bunch as well, dressed in a mixture of civilian and military clothing, I didn't think this lot would last long if the Chetniks counter attacked in the morning. Our team pulled back to some houses on the outskirts of Dubrava where a local family gave us coffee, we then got our heads down, before moving back up the line at first light.

Up at 4:00am had coffee, again donated by the locals, and by 5:00am we were all back on our front line posts. On my orders we had all slept fully clothed on instant readiness but there had been no more Chetnik probes during the night. The only firing during the morning was at people who were ambling along the road, forcing them to dive for cover. Will they not learn these people? We were relieved by fresh troops from Tuzla at 10:00am and left Cerik soon after. Back at Donji Vuksic I cleaned my weapons and got my head down. My beauty sleep was rudely interrupted at 3:30pm when I was told to kit up again, there had been a call out in our area. Apparently a ten man Chetnik patrol had been seen south of Gorice. We arrived at the southern edge very quickly but they had disappeared yet again. We returned to Donji Vuksic an hour later and went to Boby's for a coffee. He told us that local intelligence believes that the Chetniks are carrying out probes on our lines looking for weak points. The Bosnian Serbs in our area may feel the need for a route back to Serbia because things aren't going well for them here any more, they are continually losing ground.

I have just been to see Ron in hospital in Gorni Rahic today; he's being treated and fed well. Dave and Boby have been called to a meeting, which sounds like work again soon, a pity, the way I feel at the moment as a few days off would suit me fine. Today is the 2nd September, a maximum of twenty eight-days to do. Gaston left us today for Zagreb and home. I was at Gorni Rahic and I missed him but he's left his address in Paris for me. I'm also going home soon, so I don't want to tempt fate by agreeing to do any more crazy stunts, in fact this village will do me until I go home. I don't want to be killed or injured; now I'm on short time.

It seems strange to think that it was only three months ago that I left England, Tom is also contemplating leaving earlier than planned but he's not sure when yet. It's a pity; he really has changed for the better in my opinion, gone are his cowboy ways, he's becoming more professional every day, I now like working with him. I keep telling him that he might even make the grade as a British soldier one day, but that's our Legion v British Army banter. He tells me that I'm going downhill, not as far down as Legionnaire though I hope. I think the deaths of John and Brale have affected him. As with all of us, the thought that; 'it can't happen to me', has gone, with two of us dead and three wounded in two weeks maybe it could happen! A panic started again at 9:45pm and we kitted up once more. We stayed on alert in full kit until 2:00am in the morning, there had been a large fire fight going off in the Gorice area. We were told later in the morning that the Chetniks had once again probed our lines south of Gorice. This time they had been driven off by small arms fire and rifle grenades from well organised defences. For once we weren't needed, so I went to bed at 2:00am when the panic seemed to be over. Just before midday Lars came by with the surprising news that the Bijela team was leaving shortly, maybe even in the next few days, and he wanted to know if any of our team were going to join them. I don't know whether to go or stick out the twenty-seven days, I'll wait and see if anybody from here goes, though I think Tom and Dave may go. Ron is still in hospital , Radek is waiting like myself, Nikolas is back working, with his arm in a sling, with Francois' team now that Gaston has gone. If I do leave I would like to go with Broadmoor who I arrived here with all that time ago. I have beaten Radek twice at chess today; he is not a happy Czech. I got the address of John's family today in Stoke-on-Trent so I can write to them if I get home OK. Lars turned up again this evening with a bottle of brandy, and I stayed up till 1:00am drinking with him and Dave, I nearly broke my rule, but I managed to stay sober and boring!

A black Friday today. Last night, while under the influence of alcohol, Dave told Boby that all our team would soon be leaving. This news has disturbed him a bit, as the villagers here feel safer with us 'strangers' around. Francois has turned up with Nikolas to see if Dave and the team would stay on a bit longer. The news has obviously reached the upper echelons which is why Francois is here. The conversation was in French but I caught enough of it to understand. I'm still unsure whether we are going or not, I do know that suddenly new uniforms have arrived along with camouflage body warmers. We have been given an allowance of Bosnian money, and we have been told we have leave passes for tomorrow to go to Srebrenik. Unfortunately I have heard that some of this money has been donated by the locals, these people have nothing as it is and I want none of it, especially if this has come about because someone drank too much last night. Poor Boby has been running round trying to please us all day, the locals here have been good to us and I don't like putting them out, and I don't want to spend their money in Srebrenik. I am one of those who came here expecting no payment. Obviously, if I got paid when I got back to Zagreb I would take it, but if I didn't it wouldn't bother me. A train ticket home would be fine, today stinks and I'm not proud to be part of it!

I was sick during the night and again this morning. I had the perfect excuse to miss the Srebrenik trip without any arguments - Thank you God! They set off at 9:30am and left me to it. It has been raining all day so I stayed inside and cleaned my rifles and read my book. It has been a quiet day and I have actually enjoyed it. So has Dog, he has been curled up in an armchair in John's room all day. He isn't usually allowed in the house but I've let the flea ridden hound in, out of the rain. At 6:30pm Lars and Andreas turned up and we discussed leaving. I have decided to go with the first group to leave. Enough is enough, and I know that we have undoubtedly helped to turn the tide in this area. The team came back just after ten, all except Radek seemed to have had a good days drinking. It took a while for Tom to get round the table in the hallway!

20.

It was a week ago today that we buried John. We have not been involved in any action since Monday, and the whole area seems to have settled now that Cerik has fallen to us, I just hope it stays that way. Boby is still trying to pressure us into staying, this morning he has been around and given us each 100 Deutschmarks (£34) and has promised more at the end of this month. I now have 300DM with the two hundred from the shared money found on dead Chetniks in Cerik. So if the worst comes to the worst and I don't get my promised train fare I can still get home, just about.

News in today is that Francois was wounded this morning clearing one of our own minefields. The minefield was placed to stop Chetniks advancing but was now behind our lines, so HQ asked the Jagodnjak team to move them to a forward area. While they were doing this an anti-personnel mine was detonated, one of the team was hit in the leg; another in the back of the head, both shrapnel wounds neither of them serious. Francois was hit in the kouratz (his Willy!), again not serious but I bet it brought tears to his eyes. Lars has gone back to Bijela to tell the lads the promise of money stories, the squeeze is on. I have been looking at the list of foreigners here. The Scottish guy killed in Brcko, John and Brale all dead. Seven of this group wounded at one time or another. It is a heavy casualty rate for any unit. Boby popped around again this evening, we are to get another 150DM in the morning. Got a message the next morning that the Bijela team are to leave on the next convoy out. Boby is going to see them; he asked if we wanted to go with him. I got half an hour to get showered, throw the kit that I wanted into my Bergen, get dressed and onto the truck.

At Bijela, we found Joe and Andy, but they were still waiting for news of a convoy south. I decided to stop at Bijela. I said my goodbyes to Tom and Radek.

Myself and my good friend Radek parting company.

Now in Bijela, I went down with Joe to the HQ for our release papers. We told them at HQ to also prepare release papers for Broadmoor, Andreas, Lars and Gary. They are in Srebrenik at the moment. Joe and I hitched it into Srebrenik with the documents in the afternoon. We also heard some interesting news this morning. The 'Special unit' we have been involved against, the Chetnik 'Tigers' that had been deployed in the Podbari, Cerik and Dubrava areas have gone having lost ten of their number killed, and as many wounded. It was these troops, responsible for the two ambushes against us, one of which John died in. Such a pity that they left in boxes. We found Broadmoor in a bar and joined him, we are sleeping in the police barracks tonight. Gary has cracked up again, he is a bit odd; he sat outside the bar crying. I tried to ask him why, but I didn't find out, he's done this type of thing before. Joe wants to shoot him under the excuse of racial cleansing. He told him he would, if he told anyone he was English.

On Wednesday 9th September I was officially released from 108 Brigade HVO and free to make our way home. Lars has not yet turned up. We were interviewed this morning by the local TV station in Srebrenik and I told the reporter what I felt but I did wonder, why the interview now, when we're leaving. While the interview was being taped, the air raid sirens went off and we had to retire downstairs. The sirens went off twice more throughout the morning. They can't bomb me now, I'm going home. Later in the afternoon, the five of us, Broadmoor, Joe, Andreas, Gary and myself were told of a convoy leaving from Tuzla, so we hitched the 40 kilometres to Tuzla on a vegetable truck and we dropped off at the Bosnian Army (Armija BIH) HQ there. We were not made too welcome when we first arrived at this large army base, they seemed to distrust us, as foreigners serving in the Croatian HVO. Our weapons were asked for, then we were shown to a room and told to stay put, I felt very uneasy about being disarmed here. The Bosnians are our supposed allies but I have already heard words about this alliance becoming an uneasy one. I hope it holds, nothing would make the Chetniks happier than a division between Bosnian and Croat. In the evening we were very subtly interrogated. One of the interrogators even asked me why the British want to fight here, when we have our own war in Ireland. I think he understands as much about our conflict there as the majority of Europeans do about this one! I didn't sleep well here and didn't feel secure. They told us the next morning that a convoy is leaving at midday; we could get on it to Zagreb, but would be interviewed before we left. I have the feeling we are being used for some reason and in the interview I told them any crap that I thought they wanted to hear, like; 'good luck in the fight against the Serbs and you will win soon!' Thankfully we left the HQ with our weapons, although they wanted to keep a sniper rifle belonging to Andreas. We said no, I had left mine at Donji Vuksic but I still had my AK-47 and intended to keep it, at least until I left Bosnia!

We were taken to the convoy start point, where the convoy commander put us each into a separate truck and briefed us about the dangers of ambush and air attack. The truck I was allocated was a very old communist type vehicle, metal on wheels, which I don't think is going to make it over the mountain tracks. We were dropping behind, even as we left Tuzla. The driver was Bosnian and didn't speak English. We parked up hours behind the others that night, having eventually caught up at the first nights rest location, approximately 50 kilometres from Zeneca. During the night, a captured T55 tank rumbled past, backfiring as it went along, at least I was not the only one who jumped out of the back of the truck, weapon in hand! Today, we heard a story about another Brit, who was killed in Gradacac while working with a Croatian HOS unit. Another ex-Legionnaire who was on his way up to the front for the first time when a mortar round exploded nearby and a piece of shrapnel hit the 64mm LAW rocket that he was carrying on his back which set the rocket off, killing him and six HOS soldiers. At least he wouldn't have felt anything or known much about it.

We were told we would be leaving at 6am but it was 9:30 when we moved on. My truck broke down three times during the day, and we ended up crawling into an old bus depot at Zeneca; me with a five gallon drum of diesel on my lap, a pipe from it was leading into the fuel pump, I was covered in diesel. We got a new diesel pump from the bus depot, but the others had left long ago; we were now miles behind the rest of the convoy. While waiting for the repairs in Zeneca, the air raid sirens went off, I watched two MIGs fly overhead. They flew on; they have probably already dumped on someone else! We eventually caught up with the rest of the convoy, parked up once more, at

10pm. Straight to sleep; another early start tomorrow. We set off again at 4am, this time the five of us aboard one vehicle, no more splitting up, and crossed into Croatia near split at 1pm and handed our weapons over to the Croatian police on the border, which meant the end of our war! We parked on the holiday island of Pag that night, and had a few celebratory beers till 2:30am. We drew a few strange looks from the civilians here, the war for them is obviously far away! We weren't leaving until 1pm the next day, so we went for a swim in the Adriatic Sea, then spent the rest of the morning in a cafe, just looking at the blue sea and drinking coffee until we left. We finally arrived in Zagreb at 11pm with no place to stay tonight; we headed for the train station. An old haunt of mine!

We sat drinking in the station bar all night, talking to two Germans; one who was a medic who had come to help, the other was trying to get information about his brother who was killed while fighting for Croatia. We had a Croatian HV (local army) soldier telling us how much better they were, than our HVO forces (Croats in Bosnia), what a dickhead! I finally told him to fuck off or I would hit him, when I found out from his other drunken friends that none of them had even heard a shot fired in anger, idiots! We spent the daylight hours looking for Vinko from the Club Brcko, before finally finding him at 6pm where he told us we could all stop at his flat. He also told us that Tom and Lars were already here, they had arrived yesterday! They had left a day after us and travelled by car, arriving ahead of us. Typical! The news from Tom was that he'd had a major fall out with Dave; he found Lars and left with bad feelings. Tom gave me the news that I was officially given the rank of Staff Sergeant on the 8th of September, the day I was discharged. Oh well, bang goes my pay rise! At Vinko's small flat, now the home for seven 'strangers', there were many things to play with, such as electricity, a colour television, gas cooker and a toilet that flushed, we even had a bath in hot water, my first in nearly four months. We spent the next four days waiting around Zagreb for the HV office at the Ministry of Defence to issue us with train tickets. When they did arrive we found we had been booked third class - thank you Croatia! Vinko from the Club Brcko gave us each 3500 Austrian Schillings and 350DM (German Marks) approximately £300. Tom and I caught a train for home on the Friday night at 9pm. Arriving in Munich the next morning and from there headed for the channel via Cologne and Ostende. We crossed the channel and breezed through customs and got a train to London where Tom and I parted company. I made it as far as Stockport where, at 2:00am, I ran out of trains and had to spend the night on the station.

I got the first train home in the morning. Of course sod's law decided it was a Sunday, so I didn't get home to Blackpool till 11:00am, but get home I did, and in one piece. My adventure was finally over.

EPILOGUE

Since I returned from Bosnia in 1992 there have been many changes. The area we once fought in, to bring back under Bosnian Croat control was lost to the Serbs in 1993. The Croats and Bosnians, who I once fought alongside became enemies and then turned on each other, which is something I'm glad I missed. The British Army arrived on the scene shortly after we left. They stood out among the several thousand UN troops stationed in Bosnia and Kosovo. My old regiment served a six month tour in Bosnia in 1996.

I have kept in touch with most of the group. I have seen Tom, Lars and Broadmoor several times. Dave and Ron had returned to Bosnia, I will mention them later, both are now dead. Joe is living just outside Gibraltar; I went to see him a couple of years ago. Radek wrote to me from Czechoslovakia, he was hoping to join the French Foreign Legion. Andreas and Nikolas I have not heard from. I met Gaston and Boby again in 2009 at a reunion in Croatia.

Before our old area fell to the Serbs, it took with it the lives of Francois the proud Frenchman, and Pelec, the brave Croatian who stayed with us as we battled to save John. I kept my promise and wrote to John's family, and along with Tom, I attended a remembrance service for John in Stoke-on-Trent, where I met his proud family and friends.

On my return from Bosnia, my old friend, the World War Two sergeant Chris Tetlock pressed me into talking to the local evening paper, though I sometimes regret that decision. I would have preferred at that time that some people at least, never knew of my venture. I could never understand the people who said, 'did you kill anyone?' They speak those words very lightly. Another question I was asked is, 'Were you a mercenary?' I don't believe I was. I went as a volunteer soldier to fight for the side I considered to be right. If I am to be classed as a mercenary then I was a very poorly paid one. I left the former Yugoslavia with three hundred pounds and a train ticket. This works out at about twenty pounds a week. I didn't do it for the money, I did it for me. Most of the group also thought along the same lines. Before he was killed, I remember John asking me why I was there; I told him I was one of those dickheads who came because I thought I could help, and that it was the right thing to do. He replied that he must be a dickhead as well! I still think about the good times we had, the laughs, the comradeship, the people and the excitement. I try not to think about the bad and sad times. It was a time when I believed I meant something, I had a purpose, and I can remember the same feelings when I left the Army. I believe that it's a stage that all ex-servicemen go through, it passes in time. Another question I am asked is, 'Was it worth it?' It was an experience I will never forget and wouldn't have missed. I had to go, to find out.

DAVE STONE

I am the first to admit that while serving in Bosnia with Dave Stone we didn't always see eye to eye, especially where the demon drink was concerned. I will again admit that he had more pressure on him than the rest of us as he was our local team commander, and had been out there much longer than the rest of us. He also bore the responsibility of the entire village and its surrounding area as Boby's second in command. Dave had fought in Croatia and Bosnia before many of us, me included, had even thought of going there. He was once shot in an ambush, which he recovered from and went straight back to the front. He then lost a good friend, Milo, who was killed under interrogation by the Serbs. This affected him deeply. As a soldier I trusted and respected Dave, his experience and expertise gave him the right to be our commander. It also gave him extra pressure and responsibility he hadn't asked for, with hindsight, maybe he needed and deserved that drink. As I said earlier, Dave had returned to Bosnia, but he found it difficult to work and soldier as he had before. The Croats and Bosnian Muslims had split and were fighting each other, and like many others, Dave had friends on both sides and found he couldn't give his full allegiance to one side against the other. He soon returned to Britain.

Britain had its own problems for men like Dave. He was a proud man, a man who had served in the parachute regiment of the French Foreign Legion and was a veteran of many actions in Bosnia. Dave was not a good civilian. No job, no money and no prospects for Dave meant an early death for a proud man. On Friday 15th October 1993, Dave Stone was shot dead in London by a police marksman after a failed bank robbery.

Dave had spent the weekend in Blackpool with me three weeks before his death. We had a few pints together with Broadmoor and Cy, a friend of Dave's from his earlier Croatian war days. I'm glad I saw him once more. I attended Dave's funeral in Watford on Tuesday 26th October 1993. Also there were Lars, Broadmoor, Tom and his wife. It was a well attended funeral; I hope it made his family proud. Speaking to the others, we all felt that Dave made his choice and took the consequences.

Nobody felt that what he did was right but we could understand why he did it, he wasn't a man who could live as a pauper; he had done too much to deserve that. What we do know for sure, is that he could have made it worse if he had wanted to. He could have hit people with the shots he fired that day. Many of us had seen him under fire; he was not one to panic. Dave did not want to hit a human target the day he died.

One of the newspaper reports about his last day was from the Daily Star. An editorial comment was, 'people can sleep safer in their beds this weekend.' I am not the only friend or relative who was upset by the journalistic crap written in the papers that day. When Dave Stone carried out his duties worldwide as a Legionnaire and when he served as a volunteer in Croatia and Bosnia, helping and protecting people under threat from the Serbs - 'People slept safer in the beds, BECAUSE of men like Dave Stone'. Just ask the people of Donji Vuksic.

RON PEREVERSOFF

In August 1994, I returned to Croatia with 'Broadmoor'. Firstly I found Boby now in the capital, Zagreb. Boby was now with his new wife, herself a refugee, trying to adjust to unemployment and civilian life. We took Boby out for a drink and to talk about 'old times', during the conversation Boby told us that Ron Pereversoff, the Canadian ex-Legionnaire from Trail in British Columbia, and who I had worked with at Donji Vuksic two years previously, was now back in Bosnia, and had joined the Croatian regular HV Army. Ronnie, at the time we all left Bosnia in 1992, was still AWOL (absent without leave) from the French Foreign Legion. He returned to the Legion, and spent his time in jail, then served his last six months service with the Legion before returning once more to Bosnia. Ronnie was now in Southern Bosnia, near Mostar, so Broadmoor and I decided to go and find him. We had, I admit, the idea in our heads, that if Ron said it was in our favour to stay, we might have joined him.

It wasn't to be. When we finally found his unit, they informed us that he was on line, (at the front) for another 7-10 days. We didn't stay long and sadly did not see Ronnie. When I was back in the U.K. in January 1995, I learnt of Ron's death. He did not die in battle nor killed whilst on line duty. Ron was shot dead as he slept in his bed; murdered by another volunteer. One who didn't hang around after the event, and who I believe was British. They had been involved in a drunken argument the previous evening. A sad way to go for such a good man like Ron. A man who I will always remember for his bravery, the day he was wounded as he risked his life trying to save a comrade on August 29, 1992.

In November 2009 I attended the annual reunion in Vinkovci, Croatia. It is a reunion of the International Volunteers who fought for Croatia. It runs alongside the Croatian remembrance of the battle of Vukovar which fell to the Serbs amid the bitter fighting in 1991. We are allowed to march alongside the Croatian war veterans. At the reunion I met Gaston, who was now settled and living in Croatia. I met many other Volunteers who became friends that had fought in other areas of Croatia and Bosnia, many of whom had also settled in Croatia. My good Friend Boby, my ex Croatian commander was also there, where he now lives in Vinkovci with his family. We shared a few beers, and one day took me and my wife into Bosnia to visit John Rowley's grave.

Me (left) and Boby at John Rowley's grave, Lanista 2009.

I couldn't believe how the area we once fought in had changed, Boby's parents had moved back onto their farm in Donji

Vuksic., and the people have moved back into the once desolate areas. When we stopped at Boby's parent's farm, people from the village came to say Hello to me, and shake my hand; my wife was overwhelmed with the people's kindness. John's grave had been upgraded by cash donated from the locals since the war, and is regularly tended by those same people. It was good to see his sacrifice had not been forgotten.

However, not all the news Boby had for me was good. He told me that my good mate Radek, the Crazy Czech, had been killed several years earlier in his home town, after coming off his motorbike. We raised a drink to Radek. Another good man I can never forget.

Also available from Panic Press, Amazon and all good bookstores!

War and Beer, by Steve Gaunt £6.99

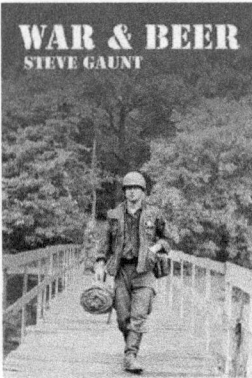

Watching the war unfold in Croatia on TV, Steve Gaunt felt complelled to take an activist role. So with no military experience at all, he packed himself off for the front as a volunteer soldier. It was the beginning of an odyssey through which he evolved into a seasoned soldier, a war invalid, and a professional photographer. During the war years, Steve Gaunt kept a diary which he dubbed War and Beer.

Paint: a Boy Soldiers Story, by Simon Hutt £11.99

Simon Hutt always wanted to join the Army. In 1989, aged 16, he enlisted in the Royal Artillery and within months his unit was posted to the Middle East to take part in the first Gulf War... ...Simon was only 17. The devastation and destruction left a big impression and on his return he wondered why the Western World could mobilise its forces to fight for Kuwait, but not the likes of Bosnia or Rwanda. Determined to make a difference, Simon goes AWOL and travels to the former Yugoslavia to join the Bosnian Croat Army. Fighting for people instead of oil... ...but the scars of war are not only physical.

www.ingramcontent.com/pod-product-compliance
Lightning Source LLC
Chambersburg PA
CBHW052033090426
42739CB00010B/1894